D1489123

World University Library

The World University Library is an international series
of books, each of which has been specially commissioned.
The authors are leading scientists and scholars from all over
the world who, in an age of increasing specialisation, see the
need for a broad, up-to-date presentation of their subject.
The aim is to provide authoritative introductory books for
university students which will be of interest also to the general
reader. The series is published in Britain, France, Germany,
Holland, Italy, Spain, Sweden and the United States.

Frontispiece McLean's cartoon *State of the Country*, 1830.

Jürgen Kuczynski

The Rise of
the Working Class

translated from the German by C.T.A. Ray

World University Library

McGraw-Hill Book Company
New York Toronto

© Jürgen Kuczynski 1967
Translation © George Weidenfeld and Nicolson Limited 1967
Library of Congress Catalog Card Number: 67-14682
Phototypeset by BAS Printers Limited, Wallop, Hampshire, England
Printed by Officine Grafiche Arnoldo Mondadori, Verona, Italy

Contents

Introduction

What do we mean by workers when we speak of the working class? What distinguishes them from others who work, for in the wider sense of the word there have been workers as long as there have been men on this earth. If we look at the social structure of any country today, we find no stratum, group or class in which people do not work. Nonetheless, the working farmer or university professor, the working artisan or factory owner, and the child working at school are none of them called workers, any more than slaves, or those with feudal obligations in town and country.

What about people who are described like this?

> Within one roome being large and long
> There stood two hundred loomes full strong:
> Two hundred men the truth is so
> Wrought in these loomes all in a row.
> By everyone a pretty boy
> Sate making quils with mickle ioy:
> And in another place hard by,
> An hundred women merily
> Were carding hard with ioyfull cheere
> Who singing sate with voyces cleere.[1]

Two hundred looms full strong! One might think this was a factory, but in the lines which follow, we are told that a man sat at each loom, and next to him a boy. One loom, one adult, one child: this is how man was working one thousand, or five thousand, years ago, or even more. Not that this means, of course, that two hundred looms stood side by side, although even that may have happened sometimes. A hundred women carding hard and singing with voices clear while they worked: this too does not coincide with what we know of female workers.

The poem from which we have quoted dates, in fact, from the latter half of the sixteenth century. It was sung by the wool-workers of John Winchcombe; he was also known as Jack of Newbury, from the town where his factory was. The people he employed were not yet workers in the sense conveyed by the term

8

'working class'. Those in the working class use different tools from their ancestors.

If we refer to official documents instead of popular songs, we find a grievance aired by spinners in 1787 to the effect that they were not allowed to leave the spinning mills during the evenings or at night, and were in fact living the lives of prisoners. The police had no sympathy with them, and had had none for the last forty years, for the following reasons:

It is the well-known life that spinners lead which forces mill-owners to apply this restraint; because they work for a time during the day, but spend the evenings on the streets, as beggars or prostitutes, and they return to the spinning mills with scabies or venereal disease, or even pregnant. In the

Left Worker in a flour-mill, from a fourteenth-century manuscript. *Below* A weaver, from Jost Ammon's *Imagines Artium*, 1586. Production before the Industrial Revolution was in the hands either of men with feudal ties or of independent artisans, but there was no *class* of workers.

crowded conditions one infects another, the first seeds of the direst poverty are sown, and the poor-house suffers unnecessary inconvenience.[2]

Here too we are clearly not dealing with workers in our sense of the word, for our workers are obviously free to move around.

For the same reason, we are not thinking of the workers at a colliery in Virginia, U.S.A., of which a visitor had this to say in 1859:

Yesterday I visited a coal-pit: the majority of the mining labourers are slaves, and uncommonly athletic and fine-looking negroes; but a considerable number of white hands are also employed, and they occupy all the responsible posts. The slaves are, some of them, owned by the Mining Company; but the most are hired of their owners, at from one hundred and twenty to two hundred dollars a year, the company boarding and clothing them.[3]

Modern workers, whose rise as a class we shall be examining more closely, differ from the 'workers' of the past because they are free and do not work with the production methods or tools of the past. They are modern in their social status, both because they are free and without feudal ties, and also because they work with new kinds of tools. These two are related facts, for only free workers could work with the new tools.

But how do workers differ from their other contemporaries?

The difference between them and those who own businesses is obvious. It is a question of property. Workers toil in places of work where they neither own the buildings nor have a hand in the organisation. They are not, perhaps, without property, like slaves: for their clothes, furniture and everything else of a personal nature belongs to them. But at work, nothing belongs to them. They are, to a certain extent, doubly free: free to move around where they wish, in contradistinction to their feudally-attached ancestors, who were virtually tied to the soil, or, under Colbert in the France of Louis XIV, to a *manufacture royale*. They are free, too, from responsibility for the means of production, and therefore different from the capitalists, who own these means of production.

Similarly, the worker is different from an artisan, who perhaps lives in the same house as he does. The latter only rarely owns the house in which he lives and works, but his tools belong to him.

The comparison between the worker and the peasant working on the land is exactly the same as in the case of the artisan, in so far as he works with tools; but the fact that he does not own the means of production distinguishes him from the farmer, just as it does from the artisan.

If we disregard slaves, who do not even own themselves, there has been, in the history of men who work with their hands, no group, stratum or class which has not owned at least a substantial portion of its tools. Workers in the modern sense of the word are the first class not to own tools.

Because they are unencumbered by work-tools, workshop and property, modern workers are the first, as a class, to be free to move from one job to another. They are therefore the first, as the great political economist David Ricardo pointed out, to compete freely with one another for jobs.

There is probably scarcely anyone – nor has there been for a hundred and fifty years, whether in Germany, England, Holland or the U.S.A. – who cannot distinguish between, on the one hand, a worker, and, on the other, a contractor, a workshop owner or a peasant, but it is harder to find what distinguishes him from a mill-worker or a journeyman. Today one even hears the opinion expressed that nothing resembling a working class really exists.

In the chapters which follow, we must carefully analyse these questions and problems. To that end, the most practical method would perhaps be to proceed historically, to analyse the social character of all those who were called workers before 1760, that is to say, mill-workers, agricultural labourers, miners, domestic workers, journeyman and apprentices, to whom were later applied expressions such as 'labouring classes', *arbeitende Klassen*, *classes laborieuses*, as distinct from the working class, *die Arbeiterklasse*, *la classe ouvrière*, in its narrower sense.

1 Workers before the Industrial Revolution

It is not easy nowadays to imagine the sort of society which existed before the Industrial Revolution. We use the expression 'industrial revolution' advisedly and are careful not to say before Capitalism, for there were in England conditions of capitalism at least one hundred, and some accounts say two hundred years before the Industrial Revolution.[1]

Everyone in this society set great store by the possession of property. Anyone who was without property and was forced to exist on his wages alone was considered inferior. No peasant or artisan would wish to give his daughter in marriage to such a man. For this reason, Gerrard Winstanley, who spoke for the most poverty-stricken section of society in the Industrial Revolution in England, and was leader of the Diggers, demanded a law against hired labour. The Levellers, who at that time represented the revolutionary wing of the petty bourgeoisie, demanded electoral rights for all free men, and they quite naturally included among free men those with property.[2]

Some hundred and fifty years later, during the French Revolution, the attitude towards property and freedom were the same. In *Les dieux ont soif*, Anatole France is quite justified in letting Robespierre instruct the young revolutionary Gamelin:

Wise Maximilian enlightened him also about the shameful intentions of those who wanted to even out property, distribute the land, abolish wealth and poverty and introduce a happy mediocrity for all. Won over by their principles, he had at first approved their plans. They seemed to him to reflect the principles of a true republican. But by his speeches to the Jacobins, Robespierre had laid bare, in Gamelin's mind, their intrigues, and had revealed that these men, whose intentions appeared to be quite clear, were aiming to bring down the Republic, and that they were only frightening the rich in order to raise powerful and implacable foes against the supreme legal power of the state. Indeed, with this threat to ownership, the whole population, whose dependence on their property was all the greater because they possessed little, turned abruptly against the Republic. To endanger private interests was tantamount to conspiracy. So all those who used the pretence of promoting the people's welfare and the rule of justice, in order to represent equality and common ownership as aims worth pursuing for all citizens, were traitors and criminals even more dangerous than the Federalists.[3]

Property and freedom were closely connected and no one was worthy of belonging to even the most radical wing of a revolutionary party, no one was worthy even of association with a Robespierre, who did not make use of 'productive property' or perhaps 'fixed capital', in the form of a house, as a place of work.

Mill hands

Let us examine in this light the structure of the 'labouring classes' and begin with the mill hands, who most resemble modern industrial workers. Here is a description of the life of a mill hand's family:

Before machines were introduced, the spinning and weaving of raw materials were done in the worker's own house. His wife and daughter spun the yarn, which the husband wove; or which they sold, where the father of the family did not work it himself. These weaving families lived mostly in the country, quite close to the towns, and could easily make ends meet on their wages, since the home market, which determined the demand for materials, was virtually the only market, and the overwhelming power of competition, which was to break through later along with the capture of foreign markets and the extension of trade, had not yet had an appreciable effect on wages. In addition, there was a continuous increase in demand in the home market, which kept pace with the slow increase of population, thus ensuring full employment. There was also the impossibility of any violent competition between the workers, owing to the physical separation of their rural dwellings. The result was that a weaver was usually in a position to put something by and cultivate a small plot of land, which he tilled in his leisure hours. He had as much leisure as he wished, for he could weave whenever, and for as long as, he felt like doing so. Of course he was a poor husbandman and carried on his farming in an inefficient way and without much tangible gain; but at least he was not a member of the proletariat; he had, as they say in England, a stake in his country's soil, he led a settled existence, and was one rung further up the social scale than the modern English worker (1845).

In this way, vegetating and existing quite comfortably, the workers led an upright, peaceful life in all godliness and respectability. Their material

well-being was far better than that of their successors. They had no need to overwork; they did no more than they wished, and still earned enough for their needs. They had leisure for healthy work in their gardens or fields, a kind of work which was a recreation in itself, and they were able, in addition, to share in the recreations and games of their neighbours. All these games —skittles, ball, and so on—contributed to the maintenance of their good health and the strengthening of their bodies. They were for the most part sturdy, well-built people. In physique there was little or no appreciable difference between them and their peasant neighbours. Their children grew up in the open country air, and if they were able to help their parents with the work, this only happened now and then, and there was no question of an eight or twelve hour working day.[4]

The source given in the note to the above quotation is quite correct. We are not talking about some idyllic journey with Goethe into Switzerland. This really is how a considerable number of weavers and spinners, that is to say, mill hands, lived.

What is meant by mill hands?

There were two kinds of mill: the centralised, and the scattered, or decentralised, mill. The former combined a large number of workers in one business – like the one already described by Winchcombe. The other sometimes occupied thousands of workers in the country, who contributed their work to a single central mill. What happened was that the central mill put only the finishing touches to a product, such as the dyeing of the cloth produced by the individual outworkers.

Marginal drawing from a sixteenth-century English manuscript. A living was to be gained in the country by spinning or weaving or tilling the land.

Contrary to Engels' description, this was the way of life of mill hands in feudal countries like France, Germany or Austria. Here we often come across peasants with feudal obligations, who were forced to spin for their feudal overlords, instead of producing agricultural revenue, while the overlord, in his turn, sold the spun yarn to buyers at manufacturing centres. These peasants lived mainly in the wretched conditions of the declining feudal system. And since conditions in, for example, Germany and France were better in the fifteenth and sixteenth centuries, and the feudal burdens not so irksome as in the seventeenth and eighteenth centuries, we find that the workers in scattered mills quite often had greater freedom and a better life during the earlier than during the later period. From time to time, particularly in the sixteenth century, when freedom was even greater in the countryside, we observe almost independent village weavers. In one of these weaving villages of Saxony, Langhennersdorf, Heitz has established that in the year 1540, for example, there were thirteen weavers, seven of whom were small-holders or farmers, whose land was sufficient to provide their food, and six of whom were gardeners and apprentices.[5] The gardeners also owned land, which they cultivated, and a house besides. Quite frequently, however, the number of homesteads corresponded exactly with the number of small-holders and gardeners. Only the apprentices were generally without 'estates' and were the 'genuine' workers as we know them,

Illumination from a fifteenth-century
Flemish manuscript. Cloth was brought
to the central mills for dyeing.

who were relatively free to move about and were paid off when they did so.

Those in the centralised mills were of quite a different order. Their number was small in comparison with the men working in the decentralised mills. What Sée says about the France of the seventeenth century applies to the eighteenth, and to Germany too, and elsewhere in industrial Europe:

But these mills must not be thought of as modern factories. Rigid concentration of industry was still a rarity in the seventeenth century, although one can mention a few mills like the one in Villeneuvette near Clermont l'Hérault, which brought weavers' and fullers' workshops under one roof.[6] In the majority of cases the factory-owners distributed the work outside and kept a number of small producers economically dependent on themselves.

This rural domestic industry was already playing an important part. In this connection, the report by Bignon, the Administrator at the General Staff in Amiens, dated 1698, is apposite.[7] For most of the mills in Picardy, he remarks, work was done, not only in the town, but also in the open country, in the villages round about; frequently merchants lent the raw materials in advance. Among the workers some were employed full time at their trades, while the others devoted themselves to this work only when agriculture and field cultivation did not provide them with sufficient work; industrial work was then only a secondary occupation for the day wage-earners, who had no regular job. What made the position of the seller or the manufacturer in the textile industry so important—as Bignon also observes—was that each article passed through the hands of a large number of different workers (carders, spinners, doublers, twisters, dyers, fullers, spoolers, calenders, etc.).[8]

It follows that in the centralised mills the workers were all professionals, and produced industrial goods under the most rigorously supervised working conditions. In France, the workers lived chiefly in works hostels, particularly in the royal factories. 'The workers of innumerable royal mills lived entirely in their place of work, like soldiers in barracks, and left them only on festival days.'[9] Others talk about the 'monastic austerity' of their living conditions; times for work, meals, prayers and sleep were all laid down.

y commence le vir.e liure
des proprietez des choses Ou
quel est traitte des couleꝰ
des odeurs et des saueurs
Et premierement
Sensieut le prologue auec

Below Family weaving and carding wool, from Zamorensis'
Spiegel der Menschlichen Lebens, 1477. Before the Industrial Revolution
the most natural unit of production was the family.
Right Lyon silk-weavers, from Diderot's *Encyclopédie Française*.
In eighteenth-century France, most weavers worked at home.

Yet this austerity in their living conditions seems mild in comparison with that of many of the workers in centralised mills in Germany, where the expression 'penitentiary and spinning house' was in common use. Thus centralised mills were, to a large extent, identical with penal institutions.

In Germany the situation was such that not only were the inmates of penitentiaries occupied as spinners, but vice-versa; penitentiaries were built, and prisons were created, in order to produce mill hands. The Spandau penitentiary and spinning works were built in 1686 'to improve the inadequate spinning trade in our Courland districts.'[10] As Krüger observes:

There was in Prussia not a single forced labour institution of this kind whose inmates did not work directly or indirectly for a mill. It was expressly laid down by the penitentiary at Frankfurt-an-der-Oder that it had to maintain itself through the work of its prisoners.[11] In the penitentiary and workhouse at Jauer there was a spinning works for the Goldberg clothiers, who were thus enabled to offer their goods at lower prices. So much work was expected

of the prisoners, that 'it was not easy for them to do any additional jobs.' The revenue from their efforts flowed into the prison treasury, which supplied the money for board and lodging, and for the upkeep of the building.[12,13]

There were times when the organisation of a mill broke down, as there were not enough potential prison inmates. From Saxony Forberger reports:

A plan made by the famous financial adviser Raabe was concerned with the employment of serfs by means of mill labour. He offered his services to the department of Land Economy, Works and Trade, and undertook to maintain, 'under certain conditions', two to three hundred cotton-spinners and combers at the penitentiary and poor house at Waldheim and Torgau, and also at what is our local (i.e. Dresden) home for the poor.[14] An inquiry revealed that there was a lack of 'surplus labour', and the plan did not come into being, partly for this reason, and partly because doubts had been expressed about some of Raabe's conditions.[15,16]

Compulsion naturally played its part in England too, in the centralised mills; but this was neither so widespread, nor on such a large scale, in the century before the Industrial Revolution. There is a logical connection here, for with the expansion of industry, the transition to the new 'Social Contract' was completed, while the feudal ruling classes were still looking at each other across the continent of Europe, in France, Poland, Prussia and Moravia, and elsewhere, at a time when the development of industries was bringing in its train the increased unrest of the masses, whose existence had become intolerable under prevailing conditions.

As a result, in England the moral argument for work comes even more clearly into the picture. A puritanical lawyer spoke in The House of Commons in 1597 of the 'horrible abuses of idle and vagrant persons, greatly offensive both to God and the world'.[17] Even so, as a result of the statutes and ordinances against mendicancy in the German states and Eastern Europe, and also in the west of that continent, the fear engendered among the ruling classes for the uprooted populations speaks volumes. This corresponds with the period when brutal legislation was passed in England against vagrants in the sixteenth and the first quarter of the seventeenth century. This legislation was already losing all practical effect during the seventeenth century, and was officially repealed by Queen Anne in 1714.

Even in England, where conditions were so favourable, comparatively speaking (in summarising our remarks about mill labour, we are standing by what we have said), work in the centralised mills was considered inferior and unworthy of respectable human beings; and countless young country girls, who, though they did spinning with their parents at home, were allowed to marry a clergyman's son, however small their dowry, were in the eyes of the poorest apprentice craftsman little better than beggars or street-girls, if they went to work in the central mills. The reason given for this association of ideas between a street-girl and a mill worker was that the former offered her body in public and the latter did 'public work', working publicly and not in her own home. On the other hand, this judgement did illustrate the

24

actual mode of life of countless mill workers, and corresponded with the type of men with whom they worked: men without property, without fixed homes, and, in comparison with all other employed people, with no reliable source of income. Workers in the central mills, which were forerunners of the present-day factories, were fundamentally social 'outsiders'.

Miners

To a certain extent this holds good for another main group of the modern working class, the miners.

It is by no means such a remarkable coincidence that the first European student of mining science was called Georgius Agricola. For European mining in the Middle Ages (not perhaps in ancient Athens) was a branch of husbandry, and one feature it had in common with husbandry – the more it developed and eventually became a completely industrial business – was its isolation from the town. Having developed into an industry, mining caused workers to be concentrated in particular regions and settlements – mining villages – whose mode of life was frequently, and in a large variety of ways, different from that of the rest of mankind.

The colliers came to be looked upon by the urban population as something almost less than human. They were herded together in miserable hovels in villages which were equally miserable and cheerless. They were almost completely cut off from any associations with their fellows in other occupations. All sorts of lurid stories were told about these dark and grimy people; and the ordinary, respectable tradesmen would have been horrified at the idea of social mingling with these harshly exploited toilers. In Fife the dead collier was not allowed to lie in the same burial ground as the free labourer.

That is how Page Arnot describes the social conditions of the Scottish miner in the eighteenth century.[18] G. D. H. Cole makes a very similar assessment: 'Miners and heavy metal workers were often looked on as a race of savages, set apart from the rest of society.'[19] Even as recently as the 24 September 1880, Van Gogh was writing:

Miners and weavers are a race of men on their own, distinct from other workers and artisans; I feel a great sympathy for them, and I would count myself lucky if one day I managed to draw these still unknown, or almost unknown, types in such a way that they would then be recognised.

The man from the depths of the earth, 'de profundis', is the worker at the coal-face; the other with the brooding, almost dreamy, somnambulist's look is the weaver. I have been living two years among them and have come to know their special characteristics, more particularly the pit-workers. Increasingly I find that there is something moving, even heart-rending, about these poor, unknown workers. One might almost call them the lowest of the low, the most despised men, who, thanks to people's somewhat lively but erroneous imaginations, are pictured as a crowd of rogues and robbers. Rogues, drunkards and robbers there are among them, as there are elsewhere, but they are certainly not typical.[20]

The situation was, of course, quite different for those miners who were really not miners but farmworkers. Here we are not dealing with particular cases, but with large groups of people in many regions (for example, in Northern France before 1789), who worked on the land in summer and went to toil in the mines from time to time, because 'wife and children gave them too much work'. These men were not social 'outsiders', even though their living conditions were often particularly poor. The reason for these poor conditions was that the feudal landowners underpaid them with the excuse that their earnings were considerably supplemented in the mines; and that the mine-owners paid them particularly badly with the excuse that they really earned their living on the land.

Journeymen and apprentice craftsmen

Mention must be made of probably the largest group of workers before the Industrial Revolution – journeymen and apprentice craftsmen. It is well-known that the state of the craft-guilds on the continent of Europe in the seventeenth and eighteenth centuries was steadily growing worse. Justus Möser, in his *Patriotische Phantasien*, remarks: 'In our age, there is something unfinished about nearly all German work, such as we never find in an antique,

or in a present-day English article. The craft-guilds have deteriorated so much with the expansion of trade.'[21] Möser's remark was applicable not only to Germany, but also to France, with the exception of the Paris luxury trade, and to Austria or Italy.

In connection with the question we have put, we must now give a prominent place to what follows.

There was a time when every apprentice and journeyman could, theoretically, become a master, that is to say, the owner of a workroom with apprentices and journeymen under him. An artisan was a highly respected member of society, who often owned the tools he used, and most of the ones used by those who worked for him. In their heyday the masters represented the ruling class in many continental towns, after they had driven the merchants or country squirearchy from the top positions.

Historically, though, it must be observed that this theoretical

possibility disappeared in practice for a growing number of journeymen with the decline of the guilds. For with this decline the masters began to make it more and more difficult for the journeymen to become masters themselves, because of competition. When Schmoller says that, in Bavaria, a journeyman could only 'enter the narrow circle of fully-qualified masters with a full money-bag, or on the arm of a dead master's widow',[22] it often applied to the whole of Europe too. In fact, the position of the 'eternal journeyman' stemmed from this.

Nevertheless, even he owned some of his tools, and it became ever easier for him to become an illegal master. The number of such journeymen who became independent without the permission of their guild increased steadily during the eighteenth century. The Marquis d'Argenson, for example, noted in his journal on the 16 March 1753:

Blacksmith's workshop, an illumination
from a fourteenth-century English manuscript.
In medieval England artisans were independent
and had their own means of production.

This suburb of Saint-Antoine is full of small artisans who are not masters
of their trades; as conditions in Paris grow worse because of the increasingly
disproportionate distribution of wealth, the goods made by these artisans,
which do not approach the quality of those of the great masters, fetch low
prices.

Such journeymen (and sometimes apprentices) who had become
independent, were referred to by a score of names such as *chambre-
lans*, *Bönhasen* (botchers), and so on. However, even if these
masters without guilds worked illegally, they were once again
freeholders, and at the height of the French Revolution many of
them were to be found among the enthusiastic followers of Robespierre; nevertheless they were far from being *sansculottes*. They
were, for the most part, on hostile terms with these people.

A number of craftworkers (a large number, even from the towns,
says Schmoller[23] with some exaggeration perhaps) became small
farmers in order to supplement their livelihood, although it may
be assumed that a considerable number of them, even in the towns,
had always possessed a certain amount of productive land.

The situation of the craft-guilds in England was much the same,
even though they began to decline for completely different reasons;
not because of a general decline in society, but owing to competition from the mills. The deterioration was, in addition, limited to
those trades which were competing with the mills.

In the American colonies, where mining and manufacture
played an insignificant rôle, the guild-worker's position was
important, respected and, from an economic point of view, relatively good. Evidence of this lies in the fact that the guild-worker
was not addressed as Mr and Mrs, like a member of the ruling
class, nor as a simple worker by his christian name, but by 'good-
man' and 'goodwife'. Among immigrants an artisan ranked
higher than a teacher.

To some extent artisans lived in industrial conditions reminiscent
of eleventh or twelfth century Europe, in that they were assigned to
large agricultural estates. There were plantations on which only
half a dozen bootmakers worked, together with those whose

principal trade was spinning and weaving, and of course smiths, carpenters, and so forth.[24] In addition, they were not infrequently committed in one way or another to work on an agricultural estate, like the early medieval artisans; there were serfs among them of course; an appreciable number of them were 'indentured persons', working to repay their sea-passages and mounting 'loans' in a sort of debtor's thraldom. In this category were all those whose families carried on agriculture as a main business on territory within the plantations to which they were directed.

In the smaller towns, the situation of artisans was as favourable as in the best period of the craft-guilds in Europe. In the cities (in 1775 Philadelphia had forty thousand, New York twenty-five thousand and Boston sixteen thousand inhabitants), they were not badly off economically, but they never had the same influence in the city administrations of Philadelphia, New York or Boston as they had in York, Nuremberg or Rennes a few centuries before, or in dozens of small country towns in the U.S.A. around 1775.

In any case, we can say quite definitely that artisans were never social 'outsiders', in the way that centralised mill workers or miners were; they were very much part of the scheme of things.

Peasant family on the tramp, by Rembrandt, 1652.
Day-labourers might do any sort of casual work
on the land or in the towns, but they
were only one section of the agricultural workers –
others had higher social standing.

To draw isolated comparisons between skilled workers and artisans, and between numerous workers in home-industries and auxiliaries (i.e. apprentices) is easy; to draw general comparisons is not. A centralised mill might employ a small craftsman as a skilled worker, as an artisan, or as a mechanic; he might work there temporarily and keep his own workshop, or move permanently to the mill. In either case he remained separate from the rest of the mill workers.

Workers on the land

The last main group of workers before the Industrial Revolution were the workers on the land, the rural wage-labourers. In his publication *Machinisme et bien-être*, Jean Fourastin[25] attempted a modern reconstruction of the classification of people, drawn up by de Vauban[26] at the end of the seventeenth century. The following groups appeared in the same category:

> Wage-earners and salaried personnel or artisans.
> Royal officers with a salary of 150 livres per annum (average).
> Servants and labourers earning thirty livres per annum with board and lodging.

This is a somewhat strange sequence. Nonetheless, the majority of workers on the land came in the category of 'servants and labourers', and their number was given as 1,150,000.

Who were these workers on the land? There were many of them in western and central Europe, in capitalist England, as well as in Thuringia, a minor feudal state. They owned a piece of land from which they could not and did not apparently live, but which they could not easily surrender: nor dared they do so under conditions of feudalism. Their mobility was severely restricted and like unqualified masters, they had a special name in most regions. In Germany they were known as cottagers, gardeners, tenants, occupants, peasant-proprietors, and so on.

It was often the labourers and maid-servants who were entirely

without property or effects, just as much in capitalist England as in feudal France or Italy.

Once again there were among the labourers and maid-servants some who did the most primitive work on the land, but were also personal staff of the 'gentry', and often, to say the least, reached a high social standing. In many cases they grew up in these patriarchal surroundings with the 'master's' family.

A considerable number of labourers and maid-servants however, were only temporary holders of these posts, and they later took over their parents' farm, or married into peasant families.

There were in England, and also on the Continent, wandering day-labourers who worked for a time on the land and sometimes in the towns, doing all manner of relatively unskilled jobs.

Because the experience demanded by many jobs was of a low order, agricultural labourers were to be found helping with the harvest, doing road repairs or even house-building. Agricultural labourers of that time were a conglomeration of quite distinct strata, children of by no means poorly paid peasants, whose property they would one day inherit. The servant-system forced them to have the rank of farm-workers, but they were apparently able to marry into the middle class of the population and become welcome partners for the daughters of artisans and farmers, tradesmen and propertied weavers. Or else they belonged to the dregs of society, and turned off the main highway to stay awhile on a country estate, only to leave it after a time and scrape a living as beggars, thieves, brothel-keepers or mercenaries of a landed squire. This last group was included under the heading of agricultural labourers because the countryside was so vast and afforded opportunities for many kinds of work, but in reality many of them could be classed as belonging to no trade, or even as town-workers; in the towns they served as carriers, porters, road-repairers, and so forth.

When one compares all the trades and categories who were classed as workers before the Industrial Revolution, one finds a 'group' which is just as heterogeneous as the agricultural workers.

How vastly different from one another were journeymen (who, on the strength of kinship or other connections, could be certain of becoming duly installed as masters) and wandering country labourers; or miners and freeholders who worked in domestic industry. How far apart, too, were the free rural labourer in England, who could be paid off by his capitalist master, and the Bavarian serf, who was bound by feudal obligations and the regulations for servants.

The 'common people'

In no country, either in America or on the Continent of Europe, and certainly not in England, could there by any question of one large group or class of workers.

They were owners of at least part of the means of production with which they worked, whether they were journeymen or cottagers, peasant-proprietors, and so forth. Nothing that was essential for production was their own except their ability to work. This applied particularly to the wandering agricultural labourers and a large number of miners. They were members of the same social order, more or less tied to the same territory, or with no ties at all. (Miners in Scotland sometimes pledged their children to their masters at baptism, while mill workers could work free and unattached.) They were the inmates of penitentiaries, they were serfs or even 'indentured'; they had at least semi-feudal obligations in isolated parts of England, and in Germany they were already working partly under conditions of capitalism.

They were the uprooted 'outsiders' of society like wandering agricultural workers, or firmly embedded 'outsiders' like the miners in their isolated settlements. They were the highly respected notabilities of their community, such as countless skilled workers or artisans or yeomen even, whose daughters were considered to be descending to the gutter if, wanting a change from the dull monotony of domestic life, they went to the nearest centre to work at a mill.

To those who were born later, and who view them in the perspective of history, the only thing which unites them all is that the industrial proletariat, the nucleus of the working class of today, was to be recruited from their ranks.

This is not to say that, in the eyes of theologians, philosophers or politicians and according to their class theories, a good many of these categories were not grouped together in one way or another. There were collective nouns in use, such as 'the poor', 'paupers', '*les pauvres*' or '*les classes pauvres*'; but all these people were

without property. They owned nothing at work, and so the entire group of 'workers' belonging to the craft trades were excluded. On the other hand, they included the unemployed professionals, the beggars, and the disabled and sick who were under treatment. In Seidel's opinion,[27] and he bases his analysis on Conze,[28]

The common people were, up to the beginning of the nineteenth century, the people in the lowest orders; and although, when compared with the peasant-proprietors and guild-masters, they were second-class peasants or second-class citizens, they were nevertheless of plebeian rank (*ordo plebeius*), that is to say, they were members of an order which was carefully watched from above, but not for that reason inferior or exclusive.[29] Living 'on the fringe' and often exposed to the danger of dire poverty, in need of support in times of famine and want, the pauper of the plebeian orders was by no means redundant; any more than his successor, the proletarian. From the ranks of the common people were recruited servants, day-labourers, cottagers and peasant-proprietors, and in the towns, occupants of workbenches in the early factories or in the mill, porters, carters and unskilled labourers. It was a pool for the supply of menial servants, constantly needed by the upper strata of society. It provided essential workmen and was to that extent exceedingly useful, just as its successor, the proletariat.

Marginal drawings of cripples and a blind man, from the fourteenth-century Luttrell Psalter. From a social, religious or theological point of view, a beggar was considered as integral a part of society as the king.

Thus the plebeian order in the years leading up to the end of the eighteenth century was not the scum of society, whose abolition had been almost constantly striven for. And why should this be so? The pauper had his food, a piece of ground, a cow and casual work in the towns. He formed a caste in the social structure during the period spanning Luther and James Watt. He could not be thought of as non-existent in the hierarchy of the social arena, nor should he be taboo in discussion or debate.

Seidel is wrong on two counts, particularly in his footnote.[29] In early feudal times and at the height of feudalism, beggars were not excluded from the social order, but were very much part of it; they were to a certain extent organised on a guild basis and were also, from a religious and theological standpoint, considered to be an essential component of the human establishment. How was one to show oneself charitable and merciful before God, if there were no beggars? They were also indispensable for economic reasons. As Ortes says: 'The poor and the unemployed are the inevitable products of the rich and active.'[30]

Later, however, during the early days of capitalism in England and after, also during the decline of feudalism, when beggars and vagrants were being prosecuted (they were forced to work when begging became a punishable offence for the able-bodied), they naturally continued to be classed with paupers (one has only to inspect the official statistics on paupers in England), or with the plebs or common people, even if they ranked as social 'outsiders'.

It is therefore agreed that the upper strata of the industrial working class were really heterogeneous in such a variety of ways, that they could never be classed as a unit: nor were they ever so classed in contemporary literature.

2 The working class emerges

In a decree by the Berlin government on 1 June 1819, sent to the Lord Lieutenant von Heydebreck about 'suggestions for the improvement of conditions for factory workers', the question was raised from what source assistance could be expected for children working in factories, particularly as regards the possibility of schooling. It read:

As far as the factory owners are concerned, as long as they are not compelled by bans and decrees to provide the necessary spare time and leisure for instruction, one can expect virtually nothing from them. Factory owners are convinced that the weal and woe of the whole state depend on the success of their factories, and that this can suffer no greater setback than if one small section of the works comes to a standstill, fewer goods are cleared, or the already cleared goods have to be sold at higher prices. They have become accustomed to consider the productive workers and their subordinates and children to be incidental appendages to the machines, and that it is sufficient for them, if they have not necessary energy, that their bodies do not rot and that their hands can go through the appropriate motions.[1]

For our investigation, the decisive pronouncement by the supreme authority in Berlin is that the factory owners considered the workers to be 'incidental appendages to the machines'. It was exactly this wording by the semi-feudal Prussian government of Berlin – the worker as an appendage – which we were to find half a century later in Marx's analysis, so bitterly and provocatively expounded, about the relationship of worker and machine – or ought we not rather say 'of the machine to the worker'? Marx observes in *Capital*:

Within the capitalist system, all means of increasing social productivity of labour takes place at the expense of the individual worker; all methods of developing production degenerate into methods of controlling and exploiting the operative, they cripple the worker until he is a shadow of himself, they degrade him so that he is but an appendage of the machine, his work is such agony, that his interest in it is destroyed. He is alienated from the intellectual potentialities of the labour-process in the same proportion that science is incorporated in it as an independent force; the conditions under which he works are distorted, he is subjected to the pettiest obnoxious tyranny during the labour-process, and his whole life is turned into working time. These methods hurl his wife and children under the wheels of the rolling Juggernaut of capitalism.[2]

Man was alienated from the intellectual potentialities of the labour-process and became an 'appendage to the machine'. Marx was not a critic of the machine – on the contrary! – and it was not therefore the machine's fault, but its capitalistic application. Thus:

The contradictions and antagonisms inherent in the capitalistic use of machinery exist because they have sprung not from the machine itself, but from the capitalistic application to which it has been put. Machinery considered on its own shortens the working time, whereas when it is used for capitalistic purposes it lengthens the working day; when on its own it is intended to lighten work, its capitalistic use increases the tempo of work; intrinsically it is a victory of mankind over the forces of nature, but used for capitalistic ends it employs the forces of nature to enslave men; on its own it increases the operative's wealth, used capitalistically it impoverishes him.[3]

The machine made the worker into its appendage and brought about the alienation of the labour-process, that is to say, it completed its alienation.

An independent and alienated character is given by the capitalistic labour-process to the working conditions and to the labour-product, as against the workers themselves; but with the introduction of machinery this is turned into a glaring opposition.[4]

At the same time, the alienation, the 'de-intellectualisation', of the labour-process affected people of the most diverse social strata and classes. Karl Biedermann, Professor at the University of Leipzig, wrote:

Finally came the introduction of machine labour, which forced human labour to be purely mechanical and turned the scales still more in favour of the employer's intelligence and capital, at the worker's expense. I am going to give only one example of the way in which an occupation could be stripped of its intellectual content, and it seems to me to be most enlightening. You probably know of the ingenious invention of the Jacquard loom. The special feature of this invention is that, whereas on ordinary looms the various intricate arrangements of the threads to form a particular pattern are effected by the worker himself, sometimes by special preparation of the loom, and sometimes by precise adjustments during the work; on the new machine, thanks to a simple and ingenious mechanism, they take place automatically without any interference by the workers. The weaver's work clearly became very much more mechanical; the intelligence which he had to apply before in order to transfer the pattern on to the loom had passed now, to a certain extent, over to the machine; and the benefit which the worker used to derive from this use of his intelligence was now lost to him, and rested with the owner of the machine, the commercial employer. As a result, the worker suffered a double disadvantage: first, he could now use, and therefore realise, only his mechanical powers and skill; and secondly, he was in no position to provide himself with a similar but much more expensive Jacquard loom: he was no longer his own independent master, but could only pursue his occupation in the service and pay of a 'foreign' master.[5]

'Intelligence ... had passed to a certain extent over to the machine.' Thus the machine turned the worker into an appendage for the added reason that it had taken over his 'intellectual functions'.

But the machine not only took over the worker's intellectual functions, it also became the worker's foreman. Charles Babbage, in his work on the nature of machines and factories[6] (a work long forgotten and only recently rediscovered) remarked that one of the most notable advantages for which we were indebted to machines was the safeguard with which they provided us against the negligence, idleness or sharp practice of the workers. The individual was an appendage to the machine, and so it followed naturally that the machine must be of more value to the capitalist than the individual. Anton Friedmund, the son of Bettina von Arnim – who was a friend of Goethe, the King of Prussia and the poor of Berlin – wrote in 1844 in a booklet entitled *On Industrialism and Poverty*[7]:

The achievements of the forces of nature, once these have been brought under man's control, are always the most effective, the cheapest and the most productive; where quite definite and absolutely practical operations are concerned, human achievements cannot but lag behind those of the forces of nature. This puts the worker lower than the machine. The industrial capitalist makes use of the worker only where machines cannot possibly be used, and by the financial disdain with which he treats his abilities, leads one to believe that he takes no account of the worker as a human being.

Generally speaking, the utilisation of the forces of nature is in no way to be scorned; only the way in which this comes about, notably by industrial ambition. This is its cause. It neglects the eternal for the sake of the temporal, and what is divine and universal for the sake of the crassest egoism.

At the same time, what a miracle the machine was! It not only changed the working man's position in society, it changed the whole of society, it precipitated a revolution which Engels compared in size and significance to the great French Revolution of 1789:

Whereas in France the hurricane of revolution swept the country, there passed through England a quieter, but no less powerful upheaval. Steam and the new mechanical tools changed mill-working into modern heavy industry, thereby revolutionising the whole basis of middle class society. The sleepy evolution of the period of manufacture was turned into a veritable 'storm and stress' period of production.[8]

At the turn of the century, the great theologian Schleiermacher was filled with enthusiasm for the 'ingenious machine' as being a symbol of the new age:[9]

I feel here the companionship which unites me with everyman; it is the fulfilment of his inborn power at every moment of his life. Each individual carries out his appointed task, he completes the work of a man he does not know, and paves the way for another who knows nothing of his efforts on his own behalf. So the common work of man spreads out all over the world, each one feels the effects of another's efforts as if this were his own life, and the 'ingenious machine' of this fellowship takes each gentle movement of the individual, strengthens it through thousands of others and brings it to fruition, as if they were his own limbs and all the work he had ever done were completed in a moment.

A generation later, the French literary critic, Désiré Nisard observed: 'The whole of contemporary poetry is concerned with the bows of steamships and with railway lines',[10] and eleven years

Lithograph showing the opening of the Stockton to Darlington railway, 1825.

later, the same year that Anton Friedmund von Arnim was writing that the machine was of greater value to the capitalist than the worker, the French Academy set as a subject for the annual poetry competition the discovery of steam as an important factor in the development of industry.

However, it was not really the steam engine which caused the crisis. When Engels began his early work on the condition of the working class in England with these words: 'The story of the working class in England begins during the second half of the last century with the invention of the steam engine and the use of machinery for the manufacture of cotton',[11] he was only partly right.

The invention of the steam engine belongs to the past, considerably before the Industrial Revolution. It was an invention of the period of the mills, and was widely used in mining. It did not bring about a revolution in methods of production, and evolved merely as an aid for strengthening pumping processes. This made it possible to remove water more quickly and in greater quantities, and thus to sink deeper shafts, which enabled more economical use to be made of the coal produced. With the help of steam pumps developed mainly by Savery and Newcomen, it became possible to increase English coal-production by nearly fifty per cent between the beginning and middle of the eighteenth century.

It is correct to say that the steam pumps could only find industrial use in a capitalistic country when the production of goods was going ahead quickly. When a feudal prince in Germany heard of this marvel, and procured one of these machines for himself, he used it to operate the fountains in his manorial park!

But in England, the steam engine's only other use was to satisfy the ever-present fuel needs.

Only the mechanical tool caused a revolution. It was the machine which reduced the value of the old tools, the property of the individual craftsmen or building-workers, and replaced (or 'made use of personally' or 'incorporated in itself') the accomplishments and 'intellectual powers' of the workers.

The introduction of the mechanical tool was the work of English inventive genius and English industrial practice, based on the state of production under capitalism and its requirements. It is essential to take a somewhat closer look at this tremendous, epoch-making event in the history of mankind.[12]

The introduction of the mechanical tool into textile production was really one of the most interesting events of any period of industrial history.[13] Its technical starting-point was the disproportionate development of spinning and weaving, the two main branches of the industry. Spinning had lagged far behind weaving technically and in productivity. An unusually large number of spinners had to be employed in order to provide the weavers with sufficient thread (a situation to be found both in early capitalist England, and in the feudal industry of the Continent; a situation which led, on the Continent for instance, more and more to compulsory employment in the spinning industry. Even soldiers and their wives were forced into spinning.). In 1733 the English engineer Kay invented the so-called flying shuttle system, which doubled the weaver's productivity. The disproportion between spinning and weaving had now become so clear-cut that there were eight to twelve spinners for every weaver. It is evident that in these circumstances, all possible efforts were made to increase the work

The ENGINE for Raising Water (with a power made) by Fire.

produced by the spinners, and it is not surprising that the Royal Society, the foremost scientific society in England, offered a prize for a discovery which would contribute to a speeding up of the spinning process. The first man to construct a seemingly efficient spinning machine was Wyatt, two years after Kay's invention to improve weaving. Wyatt's construction must be looked upon as the starting-point of the Industrial Revolution. However, one cannot say that Wyatt's machine was sufficient to eliminate the disproportion between the spinners and the weavers; and the machine was not yet of sufficient quality for general use. The basic problem had not been solved, and many inventors continued to be active in this direction. Three years after Wyatt, Paul produced a spinning machine, which, even in its improved version of 1748, was just as unsuccessful in satisfying the need. Only in 1764, a whole generation after Kay's invention, when matters were even

Left Newcomen's atmospheric engine, 1717. In eighteenth-century England – where capitalism already prevailed – steam power made mining more efficient. But the real revolution came in the cotton industry where alternate advances in spinning and weaving methods hastened its development. *Top* Hargreaves' *Spinning Jenny*, 1764. *Bottom* Cartwright's power loom, 1785.

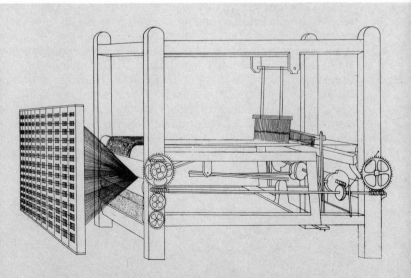

The cotton industry as a cottage industry, from *The Testimonial of John Kay*.

more critical, Hargreaves succeeded in bringing out his very successful 'spinning Jenny'. Five years later, Arkwright used water-power to drive an improved spinning machine. Now, or more correctly two years later, in 1771, when Arkwright's first machines were being put into action, we can talk in terms of factories for the first time – as opposed to mills, which were characterised by handwork. In 1775, Arkwright substantially improved his machine, and he was followed by Crompton in 1778, who made a further improvement.

Now a new disproportion had arisen: the amount of work produced by the spinners was appreciably larger than that of the weavers. It now became necessary in turn to speed up the weaving process, and soon after the setting up of Crompton's improved spinning machine, Cartwright in 1785 invented a weaving machine, which, in the course of time – particularly following improvements made in 1788 and 1789 – so accelerated the weaving-process, that at least it matched the output of the spinning-works. Nevertheless it took so long to spread Cartwright's invention that as late as eighteen hundred a conference of employers was held in Lancashire to 'remedy the shortage of weavers', and this pointed to the continuing superiority of the spinning-process. In 1804, however, Cartwright had developed the power loom

so far, that he was able to compete successfully with the handloom-weavers With these inventions, which have been improved each year since then, the

victory of machine-work over hand-work in the main branches of English industry was clear-cut, and the whole history of the latter, from now on, told how the hand-worker was driven out of one job after the other by the machines.[14]

The eighties also saw the first use of steam-engines in the textile industry, in the cotton industry, to be precise; and here again, this took place mainly in Lancashire concerns. In other words, the cotton industry was really the first factory industry in England.

Nevertheless, around 1760 and 1770, this first factory industry was still part of the country's small industries. However significant the development of the cotton industry is as a factory industry, however important it is as a feature of the gradual change in the production methods from capitalised mills to industrial capital, one must be very much on one's guard against overestimating the advance of the Industrial Revolution in its broadest context during the eighteenth century.

In order to have a clear picture of the part played by the cotton industry, that is, the factory industry, it would be profitable to consult a contemporary writer who discussed the significance of the separate industries. According to information given by Mac-Pherson in his *Trade Annals*, it was the woollen industry which in 1783 stood at the head of all non-agricultural branches of trade, with production worth seventeen million pounds. After this came the iron and iron-goods industry with twelve million, and the leather

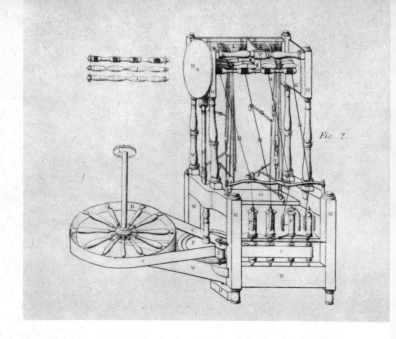

Fig. 2.

and leather-goods industry with ten-and-a-half million pounds.
Then, a long way behind, came the silk industry with production
worth three-and-a-half million pounds. Only after the linen, lead,
tin and porcelain industries do we find the cotton industry with
something less than one million pounds' worth of production.
Coal-mining, brewing, the building industry and ship-building
have been left out of this summary. But from that time, from the
1880s, there was quite a rapid growth in the cotton industry,
which can best be illustrated by comparing the raw materials
consumed in the woollen industry, still, in 1785, the largest. The
consumption of cotton, amounting to a weight of only just over
one million pounds, had, by 1810, within one generation, risen to
nearly twenty-five times as much to twenty-seven million; and in
spite of the war and post-war depression to nearly thirty-four
millions in 1818, then in 1831 to the enormous total of about
fifty-seven million pounds. On the other hand, the consumption of
wool, over ten times as great as that of cotton in 1781, more than
eleven million pounds, was already substantially less than that of
cotton in 1810, and in 1830 barely a third as large, a little over
eighteen millions.

Left Sir Richard Arkwright (1732–92). *Far left* His spinning machine, 1767. By 1771 Arkwright's improved spinning machine was being used industrially, and we can begin to talk of factories rather than mills.

Hatred of the machine

The modern working class is the product of the machine. It is an association of people, non-political and not formed for other reasons, by personal inclination or by individual entry. It is the result of the development of productive energy. It is the creation of the machine – to be exact, of the mechanical tool. No machines would mean no working class.

It consists of men, whose tool the machine is: a tool that is far too expensive to be owned by the individual worker. The worker (from now on we include under this heading only the modern worker who belongs to the working class) therefore owns nothing. Without being master of anything but his working power as far as the process of production is concerned (personal property plays no part in the production process) the worker lives dependent on the running of the machine, which is determined not by him, but by the machine's owner. In contrast with the official, the technician or any other member of management, he works with his hands, he waits on the machine, he takes part manually in the process of production.

By leaving millions of tools to grow obsolete, and making them superfluous and therefore worthless, the machine deprived all those who hitherto possessed their own means of production of their property, and uprooted them. On the other hand, it gave opportunities for non-agricultural work to all those who could not or would not do industrial work, because they owned no means of production.

The machine brought about a revolution in opportunities for employment and the framework of property-ownership, in the structure of society and the classification of men. The technical revolution caused a revolution in society. We call the entire operation the process of industrial revolution, with the machine as driving force, mobile initiator, permanent attendant and driver.

Men were ready to recognise that the machine was the central force of the new age, but those who had been adversely affected by its achievements, the owners of now obsolete tools, saw only 'the machine apart', as Hegel would say, the machine as a tangible influence on their lives under the conditions of a vast and expanding capitalism; not the machine in itself as a bringer of mighty progress to mankind. Also they saw the machine as an isolated object, not in the hands of its owners. A hatred was therefore built up among the 'appendages'; there followed numerous revolts by these 'appendages' against the machine in all the countries in which it was then being introduced into the production-process.

We have already pointed out that the machine was the product of capitalism, and, at the same time, that it furthered the development of capitalism to an enormous extent. We have also seen in the extract about the steam-pumping-engine for mines, that a feudal society could really do nothing at all with such a machine.

The hatred which the workers had for machinery recalls the fate of a most primitive kind of mechanical tool which appeared as a production tool in one feudal society.[15]

The ribbon-mill was invented in Germany. In a work which was published in Venice in 1636, an Italian abbé named Lancellotti told how Anton Müller from Danzig had seen a very ingenious machine in that town about fifty years before (Lancellotti was writing in 1579). This machine produced four to six fabrics at once; but as the town council had expressed fears that the invention might throw a vast number of workers on the streets, it hushed it up and had the inventor secretly suffocated or drowned. The same machine was used for the first time in Leyden in 1629. Riots by the lace-makers forced the municipal council to ban it immediately, and its use was afterwards to be restricted, under various ordinances by the States-General (1623, 1639, etc). This machine, which had caused such a furore in the world, was really the fore-runner of the spinning machines and power looms, and therefore the harbinger of the Industrial Revolution of the eighteenth century. It enabled a completely inexperienced boy in the weaving works to put the whole loom, with all its shuttles, into operation, merely by pushing a driving beam backwards and forwards; and in its improved form it produced from forty to fifty pieces of cloth at once.

In 1676 there was an adjournment motion in the Saxon Diet regarding the prohibition of the introduction of ribbon-mills, but 'that they should be kept, and not prohibited, both now and in the future, at Neu-Ostra, for the making of anything manufactured.'

In 1685 there was an order by Kaiser Leopold prohibiting machines for the whole Reich.

In 1719 the prohibition order was renewed for the whole Reich by Kaiser Karl VI.

In 1720 a Saxon general decree followed the renewal of the imperial ban, which nevertheless allowed anyone who had worked with mills up to that time to continue to do so until their life's end.

In 1765 there was a general decree in Saxony in favour of re-introducing ribbon-mills.

In 1797 there was a final attack on a ribbon-mill in Annaberg by corporate lace-workers.

In all these decisions a genuine machine was involved, though a very primitive one. Against it, those who were hardest hit under a feudal régime could seek protection which was effective if not complete.

As elsewhere under conditions of capitalism, in which the need for goods offered enormous possibilities for production, the

Bohemian machine-breakers, 1844. In Europe, wherever the machine was introduced into the system of production there was violent reaction against it. Here weavers – among those directly threatened by the machine – destroy their 'most immediate' enemy.

market for goods of all kinds grew rapidly, and all concerned had undertaken to clear the way for the machine.

The battles fought by the workers against the machine were violent, bloody, cruel and widely scattered, and they were naturally unsuccessful. The greatest battles of this kind took place in England, where machinery was used extensively for the first time. Walter Scott wrote to Southey in 1812: 'The country is mined below our feet'. Later on, Charlotte Brontë was to describe in *Shirley* the conditions of the period from the insecure view-point of a semi-radical capitalist. We were to find this point of view repeatedly expressed by the capitalist farming gentry, who hated industry, in their judgments as Justices of the Peace. They could often not bring themselves to act against the machine-breakers – called Luddites – with all the brutality which the law demanded of them.

Who were the Luddites? Thompson, who has recently made a new and detailed study of them, rightly draws attention to the fact that they were by no means only concerned with those threatened directly by the machine.[16] The machine was a symbol of the new era, hated on principle by all classes and strata who did not have industrial capital at their disposal. The landed gentry were apprehensive about their position within the ruling class in the face of the rapid accumulation of wealth in the hands of the industrial bourgeoisie; and with some justification, as the Reform Bill of 1832 in favour of the industrial bourgeoisie was later to show quite clearly. The non-technical minds, particularly the poets, hated machinery, just as they hated anything which 'is ugly and spreads ungliness'. Blake wrote a poem directed 'against the satanic mills':

> I wander through each chartered street,
> Near where the chartered Thames does flow,
> And mark in every face I meet,
> Marks of weakness, marks of woe.

Lord Byron delivered an impassioned speech in the House of

Lords against the Bill, which provided for the death penalty for machine-breakers:

But . . . suppose one of these men as I have seen them – meagre with famine, sullen with despair, careless of a life which your Lordships are perhaps about to value at something less than the price of a stockingframe – suppose this man surrounded by the children for whom he is unable to procure bread at the hasard of his existence, about to be torn for ever from a family which he lately supported in peaceful industry, and which it is not his fault that he can no longer so support: suppose this man – and there are ten thousand such from whom you may select your victims—dragged into court, to be tried for this new offence by this new law: still, there are two things wanting to convict and condemn him: and these are, in my opinion – twelve butchers for a jury and a Jeffreys for a judge![17]

But the butchers were in fact provided by the entrepreneurs themselves, as was to become apparent later. The owner of the Rawfolds Mills in Yorkshire severely injured two machine-breakers, whom he then left to bleed to death, refusing them water or a doctor, because they would not betray their colleagues.

The important thing was that all grades of workpeople, shoe-makers and miners, small tradesmen, tailors, butchers, carpenters, none of them threatened by the machine, were on the side of the weavers and spinners who were being deprived of their regular livelihood; for they were reactionary and conservative in outlook – humble citizens, for whom anything new was sinister – and they were afraid of what the future might hold in store. By their side stood a small number of revolutionaries, also drawn from every grade, for whom machine-breaking seemed a convenient starting-point for an attack on the whole system. These were often men who looked far ahead, dearly hoping to be able to combine an uprising against the machine with a political rebellion against the palatial homes of the wealthy.

But whether it involved a petty bourgeoisie (anti-progress and anxious to secure a reactionary future for themselves as artisans), workers who directed their hatred on to the machine, or revolu-tionaries; they either struck so suddenly, or were so secretive about their preparations, that the government was powerless when first faced with this machine-breaking. The Duke of Newcastle complained in December 1811:

the grand difficulty, is the almost impossibility of obtaining information respecting the movements and intentions of the rioters, everything is so well organised among them, and their measures are conducted with such secrecy, added to which no one dares to impeach for fear of his life, that it is scarcely possible to detect them. . . . A sort of negotiation is now carrying on between committees formed of delegates from the discontented frame-work knitters . . . and the hosiers and masters.[18]

We must now study a report from France which in many ways reminds one of the atmosphere of cooperation and companionship in England:

When, in 1819, two manufacturers in Vienne (Isère) were about to introduce a mechanical device for shearing cloth, the shearing-masters raised an objection and addressed a petition to the mayor, in which they pointed out that the machines needed only four men to work them. They would shear and finish a thousand ells of cloth in twelve hours, thereby putting numerous workers out of a job. When the machines arrived from Lyon under police guard, the workers prepared to break open the packing-cases in order to smash up the machinery. The military were forced to attack, the ring-leaders were arrested, but twice acquitted by a Grenoble jury: public opinion was on their side.[19]

Machine-breakers were to be found anywhere machinery was introduced: in England, Germany, France, Belgium, Northern Italy and elsewhere, but relatively little in the United States, for there there was a shortage of labour, and in any case, the number of those whose main employment was domestic spinning or weaving was relatively small.

In countries where semi-feudal conditions prevailed at the time machines were introduced (as in most parts of Germany, for example) working people often had another important ally in their struggle against the machines: the authorities. They came out with all kinds of bureaucratic pronouncements against the setting up of machinery, in veiled and ambiguous terms. A Saxon business-man complained to his king in a petition of 11 May 1811, that the town-council of Plauen had forbidden him to set up a mech-anical spinning works:

for what, I may say, is a rather strange excuse, that these spinning machines would be a fire hazard for the town. It is quite inconceivable that a spinning machine would be a fire risk, because the machinery is set in motion not by fire, but by a yoke of oxen or horses, and even if the bobbins are set working by human hands, there is still no question of fire.[20]

An Aachen factory owner, Wilhelm Beuth, also wrote a letter to the director of the industrial department of the finance ministry on 11 January 1829; it was very characteristic:

Our council, or rather the inspector of hydraulics, who had been appointed to make a report, Herr Roessler, explained to me briefly that no one would receive permission to drive his factory by high pressure steam-engine. Coming after an unfortunate incident a few weeks ago here in the Cockerill works (the bursting of a steam boiler made of sheet brass an eighth of an inch thick), the opinion here expressed – and it is being just as loudly expressed by most members of our government – is causing all of us manu-facturers a good deal of concern, seeing that already eight or ten factories have completed their preparations for the setting-up of these machines, and in all fairness no factory owner could be blamed if he began assembling a steam-engine of this kind before he had actually obtained the necessary permission, since there is a considerable time-lag between the request for a concession and its approval; and so steps have to be taken to be ready for work the moment the permission arrives, in order to avoid experiencing still longer delays. At least one year is necessary, but the fact that no permission, not even a decision, is given nowadays (this has been my own experience, for I applied to our council for permission on 25 April 1825) must in-evitably have a deleterious effect on industry. It will need an almost passion-ate delight in speculation to bring its plans to fruition, if it is constantly at war with the public authorities.[21]

It was truly a tragedy of progress in a semi-feudal land that it would 'need an almost passionate delight in speculation' to build and introduce machinery.

Condition of the working class

It was the machine which created the working class. The truly modern workers were therefore those in factories. Or, put another way, if we interpret the expression 'working class' more widely and include miners and building workers, factory workers formed the nucleus of the industrial proletariat, the nucleus of the working class.

Let us examine this nucleus more closely and imagine ourselves at the exit of a factory. Villermé, a member of the *Académie de Médicine* and the *Académie des Sciences Morales et Politiques*, one of the greatest students of the condition of workers in France during the Industrial Revolution, has given the following account:

One should see them coming into the town every morning and leaving it every evening. Among them are large numbers of women, pale, starving, wading barefoot through the mud ... and young children, in greater numbers than the women, just as dirty, just as haggard, covered in rags, which are thick with the oil splashed over them as they toiled by the looms.[22]

'These children', as Victor Hugo describes them, 'without a single smiling face among them.[23]

At almost the same time we find in a report on the American National Trades Union Convention a description which was made at the same vantage-point in the textile town of Lowell:

It is enough to make one's heart ache, to behold these degraded females, as they pass out of the factory – to mark their wan countenances, their woe-stricken appearance. These establishments are the present abode of wretchedness, disease and misery.[24]

At about the same time, Dr Hawkins gave the following testimony before a Royal Commission on the condition of the workers in Manchester:

I believe that most travellers are struck by the lowness of stature, the leanness and the paleness which present themselves so commonly to the eye at Manchester, and above all, among the factory classes ... I must confess that all the boys and girls brought before me from the Manchester mills

had a depressed appearance, and were very pale. In the expression of their faces lay nothing of the usual mobility, liveliness and cheeriness of youth.[25]

Even allowing for the fact that all three of these observers, who come from such different social surroundings, are doctors, how similar these descriptions are! What is astonishing is the impression that the contemporary proletariat consisted primarily of women and children. The report by the Committee on Education in the State of Massachusetts even goes so far as to talk about women and children in connection with the factories in the United States, as if men played no part at all.[26] And yet this was almost exactly the case. The vast majority of the proletariat who worked with

Oliver at the workhouse asking for
'more', a Cruikshank drawing for
Oliver Twist. The other children are
astonished at Oliver's request: they
simply accept that they go hungry.

machines were women and children. Only towards the end of the
Industrial Revolution did the number of male workers become
proportionate and relatively strong.

Very frequently, even humane-minded men thought that a
special advantage of the machine was that it enabled industry to
have female labour and especially child-labour. Here then was the
situation in the United States. Edith Abbott, the famous student of
women's social conditions, wrote:

The employment of children in the early factories was regarded from much
the same point of view as the employment of women. Philanthropists who
still cherished colonial traditions of the value of an industrious childhood,
supported statesmen and economists in warmly praising the establishment
of manufactures because of the new opportunities of employment for
children. They pointed out the additional value that could be got from the
six hundred thousand girls in the country, between the ages of ten and
sixteen, most of whom were 'too young or too delicate for agriculture', and
in contrast called attention to the 'vice and immorality' to which children
were 'exposed by a career of idleness'.[27]

Even in eighteen hundred Noah Webster wrote that there were all
over the country badly educated children, clothed in rags, whose
condition would be improved if they could find employment in
the textile industry.[28] And in 1808 the Connecticut parliament
declared that Colonel Humphreys, by constructing a factory, 'had
put the energies of women and children to good use.' As a reward
for this, his textile factory was exempted from all taxation, and he
himself thought quite seriously that he had rescued the children he
employed from poverty and an eventual life of crime.

The development of an ideology of this sort was, of course,
essential if one was to lead an undisturbed inner life, in which
one's religious and political conscience was to a certain extent at
peace when one saw factory personnel, or when one heard reports
on their condition. More especially was this so because such
reports did not as a rule penetrate the ranks of the ruling class,
and then only occasionally.

Some statistics about the composition of personnel in American industries follow, graded according to sex. In the cotton industry of six New England states and in New York, New Jersey, Pennsylvania, Delaware, Maryland and Virginia (that is, practically speaking, in the whole cotton industry) approximately three-fifths of all employees in 1831 were women[29]; there was in the cotton-manufacturing town of Lowell, in 1833, a total of twelve hundred male and three thousand eight hundred female factory workers available.[30] Almost as significant as the constantly increasing percentage of female employees was the rapid spread of child-labour. An investigation into the extent of child-labour in Paterson, N.J. in 1832 revealed, for example, that about one-sixth of all employees in the industry were under sixteen years old.[31] And in many other textile towns, the percentage was as high or even higher. Parents were forced to send their children to work as a result of low wages and because they themselves were threatened with dismissal. We read in a report on the situation in Philadelphia:

We have known many instances where parents who are capable of giving their children a trifling education one at a time, deprived of that opportunity by their employer's threats, that if they did take one child from their employ (a short time for school), such a family must leave the employment – and we have even known these threats put into execution.[32]

In this way entrepreneurs recruited a very large number of children, who often had to work for a wage which did not even represent decent pocket money, but whose great advantage lay in keeping wage-costs down, and in considerably reducing the average wages paid to workers.

Workers with many children were given preference in the matter of employment. A frequent advertisement, as in the Rhode Island *Manufacturers' and Farmers' Record* of 4 May 1820, went as follows:

'Wanted, family from five to eight children capable of working in a cotton mill.'[33]

What was the position in England? Table 1 gives statistics for employment in the cotton industry in England for the same period.

Table 1. Employment in the cotton industry in England, 1835[34]

	Men	Women	Youths*	Children
England	50,675	53,410	53,843	24,164
Wales	250	458	354	89
Scotland	6,168	12,403	10,442	4,082
Ireland	960	1,553	847	436
Total	58,053	67,824	65,486	28,771

* Between the ages of 13 and 18.

Men comprised hardly more than a quarter of the work-force. Can one wonder that questions were asked. A resolution made at a public meeting in Leeds was printed in the *Leeds Intelligencer* of 29 October 1831:

That a restrictive act would tend materially to equalise and extend labour, by calling into employment many male adults who are a burden on the public, who, though willing and ready to work, are obliged, under the existing calamitous system, to spend their time in idleness, whilst female children are compelled to labour from twelve to sixteen hours per day.

Gerlach adds:

In reality, conditions in Lancashire had, as a result of the industrial upheaval, often caused husbands to take over the duties of the household, and wife and children were the breadwinners at the factory.[35]

No wonder either that, as in the U.S.A., a similar ideological apologia for female and child labour was to be found in England, from which only one biological exception need be quoted. The preference for children in factories was based by A. Ure in 1835 in his *Philosophy of Manufactures* on that fact that 'it is found nearly impossible to convert persons past the age of puberty into useful factory hands, whether they came from agriculture or handcrafts.'[36]

To the main lines of argument indicated in the examination of the American ideology, the German apologia adds one more exception, to a certain extent a constitutional one. If one was intending to think constitutionally about seriously limiting child-labour, one would have to take note of the following:

There are still thousands of parents who do not have enough strength for work, or who cannot find sufficient work; for them, their children help to earn part of their livelihood. Would it not be more than harsh to refuse these parents the right of using their children's ability to work? And there are thousands of other families where there is no bread-winner at all, and where the widow has nothing but the children left to her, whom she cannot support all on her own. Would it not be cruel to say to this widow: 'You may not send your children to the factories, nor may you expect them to support you with their labour?' If the state has the right, it must also recognise its duty to give work to the workless, and help those incapable of work. But the state cannot do this.[37]

If the state made the children 'unemployed', the state would have to support them too; and it could not. Therefore it should not make them unemployed by introducing any sort of limitation to child-labour.

In this connection the opposite point of view by Carlyle may be mentioned. He demanded, through society and the state, a kind of arrangement of work for the unemployed, and in particular for men displaced by women and children:

The master of horses, when the summer labour is done, has to feed his horses through the winter. If he said to his horses: 'Quadrupeds, I have no longer work for you; but work exists abundantly over the world: are you ignorant (or must I read you Political Economy Lectures) that the Steam-engine always in the long run creates additional work? Railways are forming in one quarter of the world, canals in another, much cartage is wanted; somewhere in Europe, Asia, Africa or America, doubt it not, ye will find cartage; go and seek cartage, and good go with you!' They, with protrusive upper lip, snort dubious; signifying that Europe, Asia, Africa and America lie somewhat out of their beat; that what cartage may be wanted there is not too well known to them. *They* can find no cartage. They gallop distracted along highways, all fenced in to the right and to the left. Finally, under pains of hunger, they take to leaping fences; eating foreign property, and – we know the rest.[38]

In the thirteenth chapter of the first volume of *Capital*, Marx begins his argument about the 'personal effect of mechanised industry on the worker' with these words:

In so far as machinery makes muscle-power useless, it is a means of using workers without muscle-power or the physically immature who, nevertheless, are more supple. Female and child labour was therefore the first word in the capitalist use of machinery! This powerful substitute for work and workers was immediately turned into a means of increasing the number of wage-earners, by enrolling all the members of the worker's family, making no distinction of age or sex, under the direct control of capital.

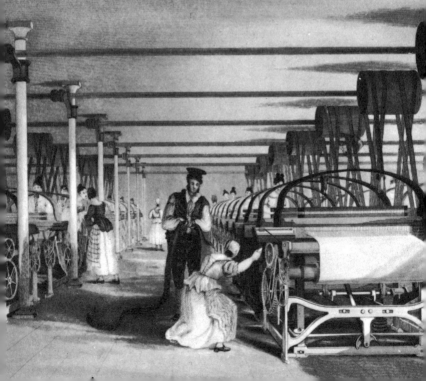

Compulsory work for the capitalists not only usurped the place of children's playtime, but also replaced work freely given in the domestic circle, which was, within decent limits, carried on for the family itself.[39]

Thus the machine did not only create the modern proletariat: it also laid down its exact structure.

We spoke above about the great predominance of women and children in the industrial labour-force. This was quite clearly one outcome of the use of machinery. Marx took this line too. But where was the minority of the menfolk? What were they doing?

In *The Age of Revolution 1789–1848*, Eric Hobsbawm informs us:

Out of all workers in the English cotton mills in 1834–47 about one-quarter were adult men, over half women and girls, and the balance, boys below the age of eighteen. Another common way of ensuring labour discipline, which reflected the small-scale, piece-meal process of industrialisation in this early phase, was subcontract or the practice of making skilled workers the actual employers of their unskilled helpers. In the cotton industry, for instance, about two-thirds of the boys and one-third of the girls were thus 'in the direct employ of operatives' and hence more closely watched, and outside the factories proper such arrangements were even more widespread. The subemployer, of course, had a direct financial incentive to see that the hired help did not slack.[40]

The subemployers, who were skilled workers, were predominantly men who had formerly been handloom weavers.

A further insight into the position of these skilled workers was given by the wage-table of two wool-factories in Züllichau in the administrative district of Frankfurt-an-der-Oder on 5 September 1818, from which the following extract is taken:[41]

1 The wages of the higher paid workers in the same trade differ quite substantially in the two concerns. On the other hand, the wages of unskilled workers and children do not differ very much.
2 The difference between the wages paid to women and children is not considerable.

From the first point, we can draw the conclusion that the few skilled workers connected with hand-weaving were considered quite separate masters of their trades, but for the 'common workers', the genuine factory workers, there had already been laid down a standard local payment. There had been a tendency in the course of time for even the wages of the skilled men to be comparable in the same district. But when we consider how the social position of skilled workers was frequently controlled by the guild-system, even in the middle of the century, thus putting a premium on the individual worker's skill, it should not seem surprising that, even in 1850, there was already a sizeable differential in wages, not only as between the skilled and the unskilled, but also within the ranks of the skilled, based on the level of what one might call their personal, individual proficiency.

As far as we know – and our information is not reliable – the situation was no different in France, Italy, Belgium or Holland. Nevertheless there was everywhere a class of 'select' skilled workers, who were in practice still artisans, and after them a larger group of skilled men who stood out above the 'ordinary' factory workers. Assuming that in about 1835 between a quarter and a third of those employed as workers in real factories (those equipped with machinery) were men, then some ten per cent of these men were skilled and 'select'. The vast majority of the men were no more skilled than the women and were counted as factory workers in the sense in which we shall now consider them as we investigate their origin.

The 'select' workers did not come into this category; they originated for the most part from hand-weaving or domestic industry. But where did the majority of unskilled men, women and children come from? Just after the Second World War, this question again occupied people's minds, particularly as it affected England. Michel has this to say:

The hardest task was the immediate organisation of the factory industry, which was something new. Small craftsmen in domestic industry refused to leave their homes to go into the factories; for this was to demean oneself socially. So factory workers had to be recruited from elsewhere, merely as *homines novi*. As has already been mentioned, only a minute proportion

...kers in a calico-printing works. These
...ly held by men. Each country
...elect workers whose origins
...ose of ordinary factory
...ted only a tiny

69

of them came from hand-weaving; in the main they were recruited from the former rural domestic manufacturers who had given up farming, from rural workers and farmers; and finally from children and workers who were allotted from poor-houses and orphanages. After the Napoleonic wars, soldiers disbanded from Wellington's army came in their thousands. Thus the first generation of the factory worker-force consisted really of the 'dregs of all classes'.[42]

Redford supplements Michel's evidence in many particulars:

Down to the end of the eighteenth century, the established textile workers under the domestic system had no strong inducement to go into the new factories; and there was a prevalent feeling that factory work was not respectable. The early factory workers were, therefore, necessarily recruited

Drawing the retorts at
the Great Gas Light
Establishment, London, 1821.

from the less stable and less responsible elements in the population. The contemporary records all confirm this impression; displaced agricultural workers, discharged soldiers, broken tailors and cobblers, paupers and vagrants, all tried their hands in the new factories, and left when the discipline grew irksome.

Again in another passage he reached a similar conclusion:

But factory work was not merely disliked because it was disagreeable; there was also a prejudice against it as being disreputable. Thus, when the brothers John and George Buchanan established the Deanston Mills in 1785, they found that 'the more respectable part of the surrounding inhabitants were at first averse to seek employment in the works, as they considered it disreputable to be employed in what they called 'public work' [as distinct from domestic work].[43] A similar prejudice was encountered by David Dale at New Lanark, by Samuel Oldknow at Mellor, and by most of the early factory masters about whom information is available. The early factory population was certainly to a large extent composed of casual and not very respectable workers. For most of their adult workers the early factory masters seem to have relied on pauper or tramp labour. ... It seems quite likely that the general disinclination to enter 'a public work' may have arisen from an idea that factories were like poor-law workhouses. Nicholls was probably reflecting popular opinion fairly accurately when he wrote that 'the workhouse was in truth at that time a kind of manufactory ... employing the worst description of the people'.[44,45]

Progress was appreciably slower in France than in England, mainly because of the peasants' victory in the French Revolution, which ensured that they led a free but above all unmolested life. In addition, the increase in population was relatively small. The profusion of uprooted families, to be found in England, did not exist. And yet Sée was quite justified in his aphorism 'industrial concerns are as traditionless as men.'[46] Men were traditionless because they went into factories, but they were not, as in England, torn away through sheer poverty, and in large groups, from their surroundings of agriculture, domestic industry or handcrafts, often whole families at a time. In France too there was something disreputable about factories.

Even in the United States of the period in question (and excepting industries where Negroes or Irishman worked), the factories were partly centres of speculation, with the risk thereby involved, and partly centres of misfortune from which one had to protect one's children.

In 1832, Lowell was little more than a factory village. Five 'corporations' were started, and the cotton mills belonging to them were building. Help was in great demand and stories were told all over the country of the new factory place, and the high wages that were offered to all classes of work-people; stories that reached the ears of mechanics' and farmers' sons and gave new life to the lonely and dependent women in distant towns and farm-houses. Into this Yankee El Dorado these needy people began to pour by the various modes of travel known to those slow old days. The stagecoach and the canal-boat came every day, always filled with new recruits for the army of useful people. . . . Troops of young girls came from different parts of New England, and from Canada, and men were employed to collect them at so much a head, and deliver them at the factories.[47]

This description, made many years later by a former cotton worker, illustrates how the stream of people into the cotton towns grew partly by word of mouth and partly through the organisation of paid agents. It also underlines an important point, which gave a special momentum to the movement: women had a special place among the unskilled workers, for the new factory system gave many young girls the opportunity to become 'independent of home or charity', and to find other than agricultural or domestic work. The other side of the picture was painted in a contemporary document in these terms:

'Within the last few years,' a delegate to the 1834 Convention of the National Trades' Union pointed out, 'the sons of our farmers, as soon as they are of sufficient age, have been induced to hasten off to the factory where for a few pence more than they could get at home, they are taught to become the willing servants, the servile instruments of their employers' oppression and extortion!' And the same holds true of the daughter who may earn a little more in the factory than at home 'but as surely loses health, if not her good character, her happiness!'[48]

In Germany and France, in contrast to the United States and, to a certain extent, England, proportionately fewer factory workers came from the land, not perhaps because the peasants had won their own property as a result of 'peasant emancipation', but the other way round, because they were still tied to the land by numerous semi-feudal shackles: including those which controlled their children under 'servants' regulations'. Above all, factory workers were recruited from artisans who had been deprived of their property, from workers in home-industry and domestic workers, from agricultural day-labourers, who had not even a strip of land to their name, from vagrants of all kinds, and from those employed in centralised mills as well. What character-ises all these people is that they had no roots and that they con-sidered factory labour to be fundamentally not permanent work but rather 'continuous jobbing'. It is therefore not surprising to find in a contemporary account the following definition of a proletarian, and this includes the factory worker as well:

A proletarian is a person who is able and willing to work, who is in need of work or of the regular proceeds of the same, as opportunity offers. Therefore a proletarian does not at present need to starve, but he cannot help being in constant danger of reverting to poverty when times are bad. He earns so little that he never saves a penny; he lives from hand to mouth and what he earns today he spends today. The life of a proletarian is thus a life and death struggle against hunger.[49]

We feel a positively eerie and insecure atmosphere in the existence of the factory worker, who, broadly speaking repre-sented the property-less proletariat, in the contemporary explana-tion which follows:

It is correct to say that the feeling of general grievance about 'hard times' is only the social malady of working for 'foreign', selfish interests for insufficient pay; of insecure work; of 'anxious' work (an adaptation of the forbidden word 'proletariat') that is, work performed in the anxiety of losing one's livelihood and one's job. This job is as uncertain as life itself, since at any moment we may die, or lose it because of a worker earning a lower wage; it is a job which is not the free and divine impulse or zeal to give expression to our strength of purpose and our skill, thereby giving practical proof of our freedom (with this self-expression the feeling that his desire for freedom is being satisfied constantly comes back to the worker, so that he gets his own way); but work which is endured as a completely unprotected enslavement in the service of another's financial interests, as the most intolerable burden, and yet, at the same time, as the only means of earning a living and paying for one's belongings, and of living the life of an animal, by keeping on the right side of one's benefactor. This is the proletariat; this is anxious work.[50]

It is clear that when men of this social background worked in factories under these conditions, the question of labour-discipline played an important part. This problem was referred to in one or two passages from contemporary and later writings, which are here reproduced. Michel continues the passage quoted above:

The factory worker of the early period, between about 1780 and 1820, was completely unprepared for his work. He was not accustomed to regular work, to companies or to discipline, nor to the machine, to which his whole spiritual make-up was opposed. In addition, he had deteriorated physically and was to all intents and purposes uncared for. These features were emphasised through the worker's existing under the most unfavourable living conditions in industry too, for they were worse than the conditions which we know to have obtained in the age of the mill. A contemporary account by John Fielden, which probably over-stresses the gloomy side of the story, reads:

'In Derbyshire, Nottinghamshire and especially Lancashire, the newly-invented water-pump was installed at factories on the river-front. Thousands of hands were required immediately for these places, which lay a long way from the towns. There was a sudden brainwave to send for apprentices from the various parish work-houses in London, Birmingham and elsewhere. Many thousands of these helpless little creatures aged from seven to fourteen were thus sent to the north. Foremen were appointed to supervise their work, but as their rate of pay was proportionate to the output which could be extorted from the children, these slave-masters actuated by self-interest, drove the children as much as they could. The consequence was that the youngsters were worn out by too much toil; in many cases they were completely emaciated, and it took the whip to keep them at work. The factory owners made enormous profits, but that only increased their greed for more. They began with night-work; the day-shifts staggered into beds lately vacated by the night-shifts, and vice versa. There was a popular tradition in Lancashire that the beds never grew cold.'[51]

In all factories and in all countries a subtly devised punishment system was introduced which was more reminiscent of a prison than of an industrial concern. In France, England, Italy, Sweden Germany and Austria, there were factory regulations, elaborately written out and supplemented by oral tradition, in which penalties were imposed for talking during working hours, for smoking, laughing or inexcusable error, for tidying one's hair before the end of work and for lateness, whistling or leaving one's bench before time – a mixture of purely disciplinary measures and unadulterated bureaucratic, personal and arbitrary torture.

From one point of view, labour discipline was a real problem. Hobsbawm quite rightly observes:

In the first place labour had to learn how to work in a manner suited to industry, i.e. in a rhythm of regular unbroken daily work which is entirely different from the seasonal ups and downs of the farm, or the self-controlled patchiness of the independent craftsman. It had also to learn to be more responsible to monetary incentives. British employers then, like South African ones now, constantly complained about the 'laziness' of labour or its tendency to work until it had earned a traditional week's living wage and then to stop. The answer was found in a draconic labour discipline (fines, a 'Master and Servant' code mobilising the law on the side of the employer, etc.), but above all in the practice, where possible, of paying labour so little that it would have to work steadily all through the week in order to make a minimum income. In the factories, where the problem of labour discipline was more urgent, it was often found more convenient to employ the tractable (and cheaper) women and children.[52]

Thus a not inconsiderable proportion of the factory workers in Europe, particularly on the Continent, consisted of unskilled labour, who had to become accustomed to a change in the tempo of work in addition to steady toil.

On the other hand it must not be forgotten that the system of punishments was used quite simply to lower wages and increase profits, and gave a free rein to the personal power wielded by the capitalist or his foreman. It also had a degrading and demoralising effect on those who applied it. The German writer, Weerth, in an unfinished novel in the early 1840s, describes the payment of wages at a textile factory, which shows the complete moral degradation which the punishment system forced on the 'non-workers':

The suffering faces of these wretches, the silent agony in their features which cried vengeance louder than the yelling of a revolutionary mob, the joy of one who hurried home with wages intact, the sobs of another who suddenly saw himself cheated of half his earnings, the rasping voice of the foreman who waved a stick threateningly if anyone was impertinent enough to rear his head indignantly like a crushed worm, the swearing of the clerks who called for peace and quiet lest they miscalculate a single farthing, the grinning book-keeper who, in his brutal, lewd way, gloated with delight over the whole proceedings, and finally the chink of money, of sordid metal, which was the reason for the enactment of this whole performance. Really, the factory counting house on this day, as on every Saturday, presented a spectacle which could not be grosser, more vulgar or more hideous if one found it in a brothel, a robbers' lair or a gambling den.[53]

And so it was in circumstances such as these, and from these ranks, that the working class emerged, that the industrial proletariat of the Industrial Revolution came into being.

The factory fused these various groups, these men who came from such different strata of society, into one unit. It was a unit which had sinister implications for other people. Hobsbawm has found an extract from a council speech by Saint-Marc Girardin which describes this sinister mass of 'new men' in their places of work and the relationship between their employers and themselves:

Every manufacturer lives in his factory like the colonial planters in the midst of their slaves, one against a hundred, and the subversion of Lyon is a sort of insurrection of San Domingo. . . . The barbarians who menace society are neither in the Caucasus nor in the steppes of Tartary; they are in the suburbs of our industrial cities. . . . The middle class must clearly recognise the nature of the situation; it must know where it stands.[54]

An English observer described this new creation representing the factory proletariat, in plain words, and he pointed out its unity, in spite of so much about it that was disunited, when he wrote:

It would be absurd to speak of factories as mere abstractions, and consider them apart from the manufacturing population: – that population is a stern reality, and cannot be neglected with impunity. As a stranger passes through the masses of human beings which have been accumulated round the mills and print-works in this [Manchester] and the neighbouring towns, he cannot contemplate these 'crowded hives' without feelings of anxiety and apprehension almost amounting to dismay. The population, like the system to which it belongs, is *new*; but it is hourly increasing in breadth and strength. . . . there has been long a continuous influx of operatives into the manufacturing districts from other parts of Britain; these men have very speedily laid aside all their old habits and associations, to assume those of the mass in which they are mingled. The manufacturing population is not new in its formation alone: it is new in its habits of thought and action, which have been formed by the circumstances of its condition, with little instruction, and less guidance, from external sources.[55]

We shall now concern ourselves with these new 'habits of thought and action'.

3 The working class: its habits of thought and action

To those living at the time of the Industrial Revolution it was perfectly clear that the working class had its own habits of thought and action. The statement just quoted, made by Taylor in his letter to the Archbishop of Dublin, is no exception, no premature sociological memorandum.

Engels recognised these very real habits of thought and action in the dedication of his book on the condition of the working class in England:

Workers! To you I dedicate a work in which I have attempted to paint for my fellow Germans a faithful picture of your living conditions, your sorrows and struggles, your hopes and prospects. I have lived for long enough among you to know something about your circumstances; I have given my entire attention to gaining this information. I have studied all the various official and unofficial documents which I was able to procure; but I was not satisfied with these, I had more to do than gain an abstract knowledge of my subject. I wanted to see you in your homes, to observe you in your everyday lives, to talk to you about your living conditions and woes, to be a witness of your struggle against the social and political power of your oppressors. This is how I set to work: I turned my back on society and banquets, the port and champagne of the middle classes, and devoted my free time almost exclusively to intercourse with simple working-people; I am both glad and proud that I did so. Glad because I spent many a happy hour in this way, while finding out how you really lived at the same time; many hours which would have otherwise been wasted in conventional gossip and dull etiquette; proud because it gave me the opportunity of seeing justice done to an oppressed and slandered class, which only a narrow-minded Englishman will refuse to countenance because of all its mistakes and the disadvantages of its condition; proud too because I was thus put into a position of guarding the English people from the growing scorn which has been, on the Continent, the inevitable consequence of the cruel and avaricious policies, and especially of the behaviour of your ruling middle classes.[1]

But many of Engels' fellow Germans were also well aware that the working class had habits of thought and action peculiar to itself, and very different from those of the poor of earlier epochs, long before his book was published or before they read it. One can even say that the German writers before March 1848 laid particular stress on the new way the proletariat thought and acted.

We have already quoted the anonymous Magdeburger of 1844 to illustrate the precarious nature of the factory worker's existence. In addition to this precarious existence, according to 'anonymous':

the proletarian is aware of his situation. This is why he is fundamentally different from the pauper, who accepts his fate as a divine ordinance and demands nothing but alms and an idle life. The proletarian realised straight-away that he was in a situation which was intolerable and unjust; he thought about it and felt a longing for ownership; he wanted to take part in the joys of existence; he refused to believe that he had to go through life in misery, just because he was born in misery; moreover he was aware of his strength, as we pointed out above; he saw how the world trembled before him and this recollection emboldened him; he went so far as to disregard Law and Justice. Hitherto property had been a right: he branded it as robbery.

We too have a proletariat, but not so well developed. If one were to ask our artisans, who have been ruined by competition and much else, our weavers who are out of work, silk-weavers, those who live in our *casematte* and family-homes; if one were bold enough to penetrate these cabins and hovels; if one spoke to the people and took in their conditions; one would realise with a shock that we have a proletariat. Nevertheless, they are not daring enough to voice their demands, for the German is generally shy and likes to hide his misfortune. But misery grows, and we may be quite sure, even as one day follows another, that the voice of poverty will one day be terribly loud!

Similarly a teacher, later to be second master of a secondary school in Rothenburg-ob-der-Tauber, quite a different type from Fried-rich Engels, wrote:

It is a far cry from a beggar to a free worker, whose wages depend on the factory-master and capitalist owner, or to a small leasehold farmer who can be driven out of his scanty holding by the high-handedness of a land-owner, in one form or another; it is still further from this man to the shabby subordinate official at everyone's beck and call, or to the helpless writer; in fact to all the unfortunate people whose untiring energy, youth and abundance of intellect are enjoyed to the full by society, but whom society pays as the mood takes it, sometimes out of all proportion, but mostly in a stingy way. They are cast aside as soon as they appear to be a spent force. Hence all these groups taken together are merely different species and varieties of proletarians.

Proletarians appear at all times, right from the beginning of history, and their appearance is always closely connected with the further development of national communities. They first appeared when people were emerging from the wild state, for at this point the predominance of land-ownership and capital began to have their· influence. Thus, as their emergence marks the beginning of culture, so their disproportionate growth betokens the approaching decay of the nation or at least great convulsions within it, and these threaten the whole establishment.

We have only to look around us at the quiet but powerful battles of the present, in which an age still hidden from us, having perhaps quite different elements and varying in pattern from those of our experience, is struggling to be born. Is not Europe like a broad Phlegraean field? The ancient soil stands firm with its states and the fruit-trees which grew up gaily out of the ashes of past centuries; but already the green expanse is splitting here and there, steam and flames ascend, and far into the distance are felt the shock-waves of an earthquake. The deep rolling and roaring signifies the movement of colossal forces which are striving to reach the glorious light of day, hostile to everything that man has cherished and valued hitherto.

Now is the age of the proletariat. They are growing fast and furiously, like mushrooms after a warm and rainy night. They have already become a riddle to philosophers and politicians alike. Who can solve the riddle? Or who could have put a stop to it in the first place – in theory, at least?

For the feature of the proletarian of the new age is that he feels the misery and the poverty of his condition and strives to extricate himself from it at all costs.[2]

In spite of the whole confused concept of proletarians in this passage, who include both 'subordinate officials at everyone's beck and call' and out-of-work writers, how powerful the message is which distinguishes the working class from its predecessors in history: the proletariat has become a class which not only suffers, but is struggling to attain a new position in society, not merely an improvement of its situation, but to 'rise above its social level'.

One more passage must be quoted, as it emphasises this new feature of the working class in such an original way. To political writers and politicians on the Continent, Great Britain was the country one should look to in order to find out what the working class represented. It was therefore only natural that the chamberlain and high bailiff of the Duchy of Sachsen-Meiningen, lord of the manor Alfred, Baron von Bibra, should draw his master's attention to Engels' book in the following way:

Friedrich Engels' work *The Condition of the Working Classes in England*, published by Otto Wiegand, Leipzig 1845, may often paint too lurid a picture, and his bitter resentment of the propertied classes strikes one as being exaggerated. Nevertheless, considering the historical evolution of the proletariat and the conditions in our country, which are in many ways analogous to those in England at a time when it stood at our present stage in manufacture and agriculture, we might be prompted closely to scrutinize the agricultural proletariat in the agricultural districts, and the factory proletariat in the lowlands and forests, in order to profit by the experiences of that great nation and to render the proletariat harmless in its infancy, before it grows (as it has there) into a giant, and threatens the social *status quo*. This we might do in the immediate future by the correct use of rail transport, prudent withdrawals from the District and National Savings Banks, and by emigration.[3]

The *Allgemeine Preussische Zeitung*, the official government newspaper, introduced a review of Engels' book,[4] which was continued in three issues, in these words:

If we recognise the critical state of the labouring classes, which is no longer in dispute, as one of the main tasks facing our troubled times, and if we ensure that the energies of all present governments are directed solely towards preventing its spread and the evil consequences by giving all possible relief to the working population in their present state, it must be of the greatest interest and of particular importance in the solution of this problem to acquaint ourselves with all the reasons for, and the full extent of, that poverty. Without doubt England is a country in which proletarian conditions have reached their highest point of development. From England we can learn what hazards a nation must avoid, if it wants to achieve power and position without being exposed to the same evils and dangers. The story of the English proletariat is for us the textbook of practical experience. It gives us the reasons for the increase in poverty and humiliation

NUIT DU 4 AU 5 AOÛT 1789
OU LE DÉLIRE PATRIOTIQUE.

A Versaille A Versaille. du 5 Octobre 1789

Left Anonymous cartoon representing the French nation in a patriotic delirium breaking down feudalism, 4 August 1789.
Below Contemporary drawing of the expedition of the women of Paris to Versailles, 5 October 1789.

among the poor population, for even in Germany the principal causes of both were present in embryo. With us, of course, the broader-based social order and the considerate use of their power by our governments are a more solid bulwark against the dangers of this evil than can ever be the case in England, but the danger is nonetheless present, and a very accurate knowledge of it is indispensable for its elimination.

Here too England was shown to be, to some extent, the classic example to be followed.

To pursue the train of thought which was interrupted above, we next study the words of a leading author in the 'Young Germany' group, the University Lecturer in the History of Literature, Theodor Mundt, on the rôle of the proletariat in modern society:

In France, the third estate continued to trail one more peculiar appendage behind it in the midst of the battle of the Revolution which it was fighting; one to which a name could not yet be given, but which one was horrified to see rearing its head for the first time in the middle of national and social life. This was the real revolutionary sediment of the nation, a gruesome unorganised mass of people who had hitherto lived by working with their hands, but had never been able to earn enough in this way to satisfy their hunger. Their hunger had now suddenly changed into a political hunger, into a rebellion against the spirit and structure of society. This was the proletariat, driven into history with terrifying force by despair over their work, and in which all the turbulent elements of society were thrown together in a blind and shapeless horde. Trembling breathlessly with all their unsatisfied urges, and forming the real disruptive force of the Revolution, they came rushing out of their hollows and hiding-places, into whose depths the new historical myth had penetrated, the myth that there was a third, popular estate, equal in every respect to the other two! . . .

The proletariat too, in which we cannot recognise any exclusively French characteristic, historically speaking, but which has its roots in Germany, represents the urge for freedom in recent history in addition to the urge for work; and the proletarian differs fundamentally from the pauper in that he is willing to work. However, now that he is well aware what work is, now that he knows that the only basis of a free society is the principle of work, he demands in return for his labours the highest and fairest wage he can!

As such concepts have become more and more clearly defined in their minds, proletarians have taken the most decisive part in all the uprisings and disturbances in public life, from their first appearance in the French Revolution up to the present day. All the silk-workers in revolt at Lyon bore on their banners the typical slogan: *Vivre en travaillant, ou mourir en combattant!*

In these concepts, we cannot fail to recognise the most important and vital question facing modern society, and its central theme. Caring for the sick and the poor is a peaceful and gentle duty undertaken by virtuous human beings, and is best practised unobtrusively. However the proletarian, possessed of this new strength given him by the legend which he refuses to be poor again, but rather rich in work, makes these most vehement and urgent demands on the evolution of society itself: and society has its own process of development to complete by solving this problem. Hence charity is quite inadequate when it comes to solving the fundamental problem of the age of poverty, namely, how the working man can avoid being poor. It is liberalism in its pure and genuine meaning, derived from the untarnished idea of human freedom, which must now lay its healing hand on society's gaping wound; liberalism, which has now, in its basic form of socialism, to perform one of its most important tasks.

This modern proletarian, this self-made giant of modern society, this disowned child of every nation, this great, proud beggar clothed in the purple of freedom, and lying so clothed on the threshold of the future, he is the true picture, the modern personification of our confused life-story always at loggerheads with itself.[5]

I have given this long extract, not least because of its lively style and beautiful prose. But only one phrase is here significant: 'The proletariat in which we cannot recognise any exclusively French characteristic, historically speaking'. Mundt was so powerfully influenced by the political ideologies of the new class, and so little affected by its numbers and economic rôle, that he sought its origins, not in England, but in France, the country which saw the greatest political revolution within the memory of men of his time, that he did not, like the aristocratic reviewer of Engels' book, consider England to be the classical country of the proletariat, but France. Here the political actions of the proletariat took place

Lithograph showing street-fighting in Paris,
July 1830. In the course of
27, 28, and 29 July – les Trois Glorieuses –
Paris was overcome by revolutionaries and
Charles X forced to abdicate in favour
of Louis-Philippe d'Orléans.

Louis-Auguste Blanqui, 1805–81, French revolutionary leader.
He took part in nearly every Paris revolution from 1827 onwards,
and was particularly active at the barricades in 1830 and 1848.
Such phrases as 'dictatorship of the proletariat' and 'industrial
revolution' are attributed to him. When he died in 1881, he had
spent almost half his long life in prison.

earlier and more violently than in England. One should not however forget that it was France and not England in which the following scene took place in court in January 1832:

PRESIDENT OF THE TRIBUNAL: 'What is your profession?'

BLANQUI: 'Proletarian.'

PRESIDENT OF THE TRIBUNAL: 'That isn't a profession!'

BLANQUI: 'What! Not a profession? It is the profession of thirty million Frenchmen who live by their work and are deprived of their political rights!'

A new class had indeed emerged. Its members did not quite recognise their own organisation, as Blanqui's remark shows. They had as yet no clear perspective as to the nature of their goal and how they would reach it – the *Communist Manifesto* only appeared at the end of the period under consideration, and in the revolutions of 1848 it did not have a decisive influence on the labour movement.

But a feeling was already growing that the working class was indeed a separate class, with its own special character and its own tasks ahead. And this feeling was shared by observers from all classes and grades, together with a feeling of discomfort or even fear among those whose own interests were opposed to the workers', and one of pride and hopefulness on the part of the workers themselves or of those whose interests coincided at many points with the workers'. Indeed, how swiftly this feeling grew among the workers that they were a class; how much more swiftly, for example, than among the artisans of the middle ages! But these early feudal artisans lived for the most part scattered over the estates of the mighty and in isolated small market towns.

The workers, however, were not only driven together by the methods of industrial production under a strict labour-discipline; and not only at night in their very confined living quarters. They also congregated in their hundreds during working hours at their places of work. In this way their common plight was brought home to them, for they were now completely aware of it.

What is more, competition too took on a new rôle. Competition among artisans only damaged 'the other' artisan, never the class, as no other class took advantage of the artisans' competition among themselves; but competition among workers for jobs not only harmed one worker *vis à vis* another, but the whole class, since it was capital, as Ricardo has already shown, which profited from competition among workers, through the opportunity it gave to pay lower wages.

Thus it was the new conditions of production, and the consequent general living standards which favoured the birth of – and we use the word advisedly – a class-feeling.

Class-feeling: not yet class-consciousness. Yet even this feeling was sufficient to permit the growth of ideas about organisation, and on two different levels: ideas about organisation for the workers to attain their goal; but also ideas about organisation which concerned the nature of the new society to be created and how it was to work. The way the working class thought also demanded a way of acting. Here is Hobsbawm's description of this process:

What was new in the labour of the early nineteenth century was class consciousness and class ambition. The 'poor' no longer faced the 'rich'. A specific class, the labouring class, workers, or proletariat, faced another, the employers or capitalists. The French Revolution gave this new class confidence, the Industrial Revolution impressed on it the need for permanent mobilisation. A decent livelihood could not be achieved merely by the occasional protest which served to restore the stable but temporarily disturbed balance of society. It required the eternal vigilance, organisation, and activity of the 'movement' – the trade union, the mutual or co-operative society, the working-class institute, newspaper, or agitation. But the very novelty and rapidity of the social change which engulfed them encouraged the labourers to think in terms of an entirely changed society, based on their experience and ideas as opposed to their oppressors'. It would be co-operative and not competitive, collectivist and not individualist. It would be 'socialist'. And it would represent not the eternal dream of the free society, which poor men always have at the backs of their minds but think only on the rare occasions of general social revolution, but a permanent, practicable alternative to the present system.[6]

Substituting Factory Rations from Frances Trollope's
The Life and Adventures of Michael Armstrong, 1840.

That is one side: the coming of self-awareness to the working class. But the other side is what may be called the demoralisation of the factory workers, even of the working class in a wider sense, including those to some extent undecided people who stood 'on the brink' and might at any moment 'descend' into the proletariat, hundreds of thousands of hand-workers engaged in domestic industry, artisans threatened by factory competition, and others. Demoralisation in the alarmingly wider sense of the epoch which embraced both the physiological and the spiritual life of the people.

To a certain extent everything conspired to demoralise the factory workers.

There were the living conditions. Taylor, the Lancashire traveller, as we have seen (pages 77 and 80) wrote a letter to the Archbishop of Dublin about the overcrowding of people in the factories and factory towns. People from the country, where they lived in the most primitive way, often in tiny tumbledown huts, consisting sometimes of only one room, the whole family frequently with numerous children crowded into this one room round one fire-place, now thought of the country as a paradise to live in. For in the town several families were frequently quartered in one room, and it was the same in the neighbouring rooms, to the left and right, above and below, in the cellar. They slept on straw, adults and children together, with no supply of fresh air, for even if one opened a window, the smoke from factory chimneys poured into the room mingled with the stench of open sewers in yards and alleyways.

It was not of course as 'bad' as it sounds, for in the country the family spent so many long winter evenings in their hut; but in the town the working day often lasted twelve, fourteen or sixteen hours, and when one came 'home', one was so exhausted that one threw oneself on the bed lifeless, especially if one had visited a bar between the end of the working day and bedtime. Sometimes one was in luck on returning 'home', for often the 'bed' was slept in by shifts: during the day-shift by the night-shiftworker, and vice versa. This worked well so long as neither worker fell ill.

Living conditions such as these were reported from every quarter. They were worst where factory-life was developing most rapidly; hence England had the most terrible living conditions, and then came the factory towns of France and Germany.

Descriptions of living conditions are numerous. In particular it is doctors and clergymen who have given us a picture of them. Edwin Chadwick, one of the most prominent champions of the improvement of sanitary conditions in England, collected a mass of material in his report to Her Majesty's Principal Secretary of State for the Home Department from the Poor Law Commissioners, on an *Inquiry into the sanitary condition of the labouring population of Great Britain, July 1842*. No political historian, no sociologist or cultural historian can pass this great work by.

There was a journalist in Germany, a radical democrat, whose description of the living conditions of that period is read even today as an historical document of the greatest value: Wilhelm Wolff, whose name is so bound up with his newspaper campaign in the *Breslauer Zeitung* of 1843 and 1844, that even today he is sometimes referred to as '*Casematta* Wolff'. *Casematte* were housing-blocks in Breslau. The *Breslauer Zeitung* of 5 December 1843 described the effect of his articles thus:

It is an amazing fact that the notices about the proletariat have all at once held our entire attention. We used to live so quietly and peacefully, we went to theatres, concerts, dances – then we came up against poverty and misery, and all at once we have become compassionate, we contribute money, we visit *casematte*.

In France it was a poet, Victor Hugo, who said of the Lille dwellings: 'Cellars of Lille, people are perishing beneath your stone ceilings.'[7] These were cellars which Adolphe Blanqui described as

a succession of islets separated by dark and narrow alleyways; at the other end are small yards called *courettes* which serve as sewers and rubbish-dumps. In every season of the year there is damp. The apartment windows and the cellar doors all open onto these disease-ridden alleyways, and in the background there are pieces of iron railing over cess-pits which are used day and night as public lavatories. The dwellings are ranged round these plague-spots, and people pride themselves on still being able to gain a small income from them. The further the visitor penetrates into these little yards, the more he is surrounded by a strange throng of anaemic, hunchbacked and deformed children with deathly pale livid faces, begging for alms. Most of these wretches are almost naked and even the best-cared-for have rags sticking to them. But these creatures at least breathe fresh air; only in the depths of the cellars can one appreciate the agonies of those who cannot be allowed out on account of their age or the cold weather. For the most part they lie on the bare soil, on wisps of rape-straw, on a rough couch of dried potato-peelings, on sand or on shavings which have been painstakingly collected during the day's work. The pit in which they languish is bare of any fittings; only those who are best-off possess a temperamental stove, a wooden chair and some cooking-utensils. 'I may not be rich,' an old woman told us, pointing to her neighbour lying full-length on the damp cellar floor, 'but I still have my bundle of straw, thank God!' More than three thousand of our fellow-citizens lead this horrifying existence in the Lille cellars.[8]

We have already observed that such living conditions were not 'so bad' for the factory workers. They no longer had the effect they had had in previous times, as the concept and meaning of living-quarters for workers had changed. The quarters were often no longer a dwelling-place for workers, merely a sleeping-place. The main reason for this change in their mode of living was the long and constantly lengthening working hours.

Just as living conditions have been described at length and in quite unmistakeable terms in contemporary and later literature, so also have working conditions. There is, however, a significant difference between the state of living conditions and working conditions. The former may be explained by what can be referred to as a general lack of consideration on the part of society for the position of the factory worker. Longer working hours, on the other hand, are additionally explained by the new techniques and their specifically economic attributes, which Marx elaborates at the beginning of his examination of the longer working day:

If machinery is the most powerful means of increasing productivity of labour, that is to say, of shortening the time needed to produce a commodity; in the hands of capital, it becomes the most powerful means, in those industries which it first overwhelms, of lengthening the working day beyond all natural bounds. On the other hand, it creates new conditions which enable capital to give full rein to its invariable tendency in this direction; and in addition it produces new motives with which to whet its voracious appetite for others' labour.

In the first place, in machinery the movements and activities of the implements of labour become completely self-supporting in relation to those of the worker. It becomes, generally speaking, a sort of industrial *perpetuum mobile*, which would go on reproducing without a break, did it not come up against certain natural obstacles in its human assistants: their physical weakness and their will. Considered as capital, and as such, the automatic machine has both consciousness and will by the agency of the capitalists, it is therefore inspired by the urge to reduce to a minimum the opposition of natural limits of human beings which though resistant, are resilient. Moreover this is lessened by the apparent ease of machine-work and the employment of women and children, who are more docile and tractable.[9]

Marx adds the following footnote to this last point:

The English, who like to consider the first empirical manifestations of a thing as its cause, often give as a reason for the long working hours in the factory the great Herod-like kidnapping of children which capital practised in the early days of the factory system, in the workhouses and orphanages, and with which it incorporated an entire human group without a will of its own. For example, Fielden, himself an English factory-owner, writes:

'It is evident that the long hours of work were brought about by the circumstance of so great a number of destitute children being supplied from different parts of the country, that the masters were independent of the hands, and that, having once established the custom by means of the miserable materials they had procured in this way, they could impose it on their neighbours with the greater facility.' (J. Fielden, *The Curse of the Factory System*, London, 1836, p. 11.)

Concerning the labour for women, Factory Inspector Saunders tells us in the *Reports* for 1844:

Night refuge for children. After a
working day of up to sixteen hours,
what was there to do but collapse
wherever there was room?

'Amongst the female operatives there are some women who, for many weeks in succession, except for a few days, are employed from 6 a.m. till midnight, with less than two hours for meals, so that on five days of the week they have only six hours left out of twenty-four, for going to and from their homes and resting in bed.'[10]

But if the lengthening of working hours had a somewhat technical reason, originating as it did from the change in productive power, that did not exclude its prompt justification on ideological grounds, and in a very similar way to the employment of child-labour. In this connection, and in another shortly to be indicated, it is interesting to study the arguments advanced by the Boston master-joiners, when in 1825 some six hundred journeymen went on strike.

'We learn with surprise and regret,' reads the masters' declaration, 'that a large number of those who are employed as journeymen in this city, have entered into a combination for the purpose of altering the time of commencing and terminating their daily labor, from that which has been customary from time immemorial.' They considered such a combination 'fraught with numerous and pernicious evils' ... They furthermore considered that the measure proposed would have an 'unhappy influence' on apprentices 'by seducing them from that course of industry and economy of time' to which they were anxious to 'enure them', and would expose the journeymen themselves 'to many temptations and improvident practices' from which they were 'happily secure' when working from sunrise to sunset. 'We fear and dread the consequences,' they said, 'of such a measure, upon the morals and well-being of society.' Finally, they declared that they could not believe 'this project to have originated with any of the faithful and industrious Sons of New England, but are compelled to consider it an evil of foreign growth, and one which we hope and trust will not take root in the favoured soil of Massachusetts.'[11]

Two of the arguments in this statement are significant: the first, that any free time the workers had would be used for immoral purposes and that they could not be protected from all possible types of misdemeanour and crime in any other way than by being forced to work from morn till night, and simply to fall exhausted on to their beds the moment they came 'home'. This is an argument

we also find in general circulation at the time, in England, Germany and elsewhere.

The other argument of immediate interest is that the idea of an association of journeymen could not be contrived by decent-minded Massachusetts people, but had to originate in some foreign quarter. This is probably the first appearance, not merely in American history, but also in the general history of industrial workers, of the invention of the 'foreign agent'.

The lengthening of the day's work took place at a time when it was usual to pay workers by the day. Thus longer working hours were not automatically accompanied by a rise in wages. On the contrary: real wages generally showed a tendency to fall.

It is not surprising that under these circumstances food and clothing deteriorated practically everywhere in the Industrial Revolution. Evidence of such a development is widespread, not only on the basis of contemporary accounts, which often dispensed with numerical accuracy, but also on the basis of official statistics. Table 2[12] gives an example of the fall in consumption of meat in Germany. Table 3 gives figures for fluctuation in foodstuffs in Paris (from de Tapiès[13]) and in France as a whole (from Legoyt[14]). These are of course rough calculations but the trend is unmistakeable.

Table 4 gives figures compiled by Hobsbawm for London.[15] It is quite apparent that the population of London increased appreciably faster than the number of animals supplied; and no one has maintained that the weight of the animals supplied during these years increased at all. R. M. Hartwell has recently advanced the theory that there were other markets in London which provided more abundantly for the population.[16] However, it seems to me decisive that the number of home-killings at this time in London was on the wane; this was a natural and fairly noticeable trend, for fewer and fewer animals were kept in the city. (We lack data about pigs originally considered suitable only for use in private houses.) Therefore, so far as meat consumption is concerned, one must reckon on a reduction when considering the classes which were least well-off at the time of the Industrial Revolution, and this in

Table 2. Annual consumption of meat in Germany, 1800–50[12]
(lbs per head)

Years	Prussian towns	Leipzig	Munich	Lübeck	Hamburg †
1800–09	–	134*	–	–	–
1809–19	–	–	245	–	–
1810–19	–	125	–	–	–
1819–29	–	–	228	–	–
1820–29	–	128	–	–	–
1821–25	–	–	–	–	538
1826–30	–	–	–	–	523
1829–39	–	–	210	–	–
1831–35	–	–	–	–	452
1836–40	–	–	–	–	448
1836–45	–	–	–	104	439
1838–40	–	136	–	–	–
1839–49	–	–	188	–	–
1841–45	–	–	–	–	429
1844	87·6	–	–	–	–
1845	90	–	–	–	–
1846	92	–	–	–	–
1846–50	–	–	–	–	339
1846–55	–	–	–	87·8	–
1847	77	–	–	–	–
1848	70	–	–	–	–
1849	75	–	–	–	–
1850	79	–	–	–	–

† Consumption in lbs per household.
* Consumption 1767–77 was 158 lbs per head.

Table 3. (a) Fall in per capita consumption of foodstuffs among the Paris population, 1821/2–1831.

Flour and bread	33 per cent
Wine	25 per cent
Meat	24 per cent
Cheese	40 per cent

(b) Per capita consumption of meat in towns for the whole of France.

1820	115 lbs
1833	111 lbs

Table 4. Population and meat consumption compared to London.

Years	Population Index	Years	Index of animals slaughtered	
			cattle	sheep
1801	100	1800–04	100	100
1811	119	1810–12	105	119
1821	144	1819–22	113	135
1831	173	1830–34	127	152
1841	202	1840–43	146	176
1851	246	1850–52	198	193

Table 5. Mayhew's comparison of quality of clothing in town and country.

Garments	Original cost	Town Duration (years)	Annual cost	Country Duration	Annual cost	Difference of cost
Coat	£2 10 0	2	£1 5 0	3	16 6	8 4
Waistcoat	15 0	2½	6 0	3	5 0	1 0
Trousers	£1 5 0	1¼	£1 0 0	2	12 6	7 6
Suit	£4 10 0		£2 11 0		£1 14 2	16 10

no way excludes the probability of an increase where the well-to-do were concerned.

At the same time the quality of food was deteriorating generally: on the mainland of Europe as well as in England and the United States. We only need to give one account from the latter, and then only concerning one foodstuff. Richard Osborn Cummings describes the quality of milk:

But increased use of country milk did not mean an end to swill milk, and the latter was estimated to constitute more than half the milk supply of New York City in 1853. This milk was very bad. Descriptions are given of stables within the city limits where cows fed on distillery mash were kept indoors until death. It was said that their horns and tails sometimes rotted away. . . . Unscrupulous dealers watered their product and added such things as chalk, plaster of Paris and molasses to give it a more saleable appearance . . .

And so even if the variety of composition of the provisions used by the workers ought to have improved occasionally, this did not necessarily mean that the food itself improved. Or, as Cummings put it:

More milk had not meant pure milk, and suffering from diseases carried by this and other foods – scarlet fever, diphtheria, and other ailments – was very great.[17]

To this description from the U.S.A. may be added the English poet's lament:

> While chalk and alum and plaster
> are sold to the poor for bread.

as one finds in Tennyson's *Maud*.

The deterioration in quality of food bears a close relation to the deterioration in quality of clothing in the towns, particularly to the greater need for durability which town-life demanded of it. Mayhew worked out an interesting calculation for England[18], as may be seen from the figures in Table 5. Because clothing wears out more quickly in the town, clothing costs based on identical prices were fifty per cent higher in the town than in the country!

But when the home became merely sleeping-quarters, when working hours occupied the whole day, when real wages decreased; who can wonder at the moral degradation of a large section of the workers, who sought their happiness on earth in alcohol, and sank more and more into ignorance!

So it was in all countries which became modern industrial nations between 1760 and 1850, and in which a working class emerged as a result of industrialisation. However – and the reason for this remark will be readily apparent – the distinctive features of this development were repeated in all the countries in which the process took place much later on. Here is an example of alcoholic poisoning among workers, described by Gorki, a modern realistic novelist. He wrote about Russian factory workers, his contemporaries, around nineteen hundred, when one could think in terms of industrial revolution to a certain extent, though in a modified form:

On holidays the young people came home late at night in torn clothes covered with dirt and mud, with black eyes and bloody noses, sometimes boasting vaingloriously of the blows they had delivered their friends, sometimes sulking, raging or weeping over their insults, drunk and pathetic, miserable and disgusting. Sometimes mothers and fathers brought their sons home from where they had found them sprawling in the shadow of a fence or on the floor of a saloon in a state of drunken unconsciousness. The elders would curse them foully, pummel their flabby bodies and put them to bed with more or less solicitude, only to wake them up in the morning when the angry shriek of the factory whistle came rushing in a dark stream through the dawn.

They relentlessly beat and swore at their children, but the fighting and drunkenness of young people was accepted as a matter of course – when fathers had been young, they too had fought and caroused, and their mothers and fathers had beaten them in their turn. Life had always been like that. The turbid stream of the years kept flowing on and on, slowly and evenly, clamped to an unchanging course by age-old habits of thinking and behaving. Nor had anyone the slightest desire to introduce any change.[19]

From Wuppertal, in the centre of which are the textile towns of Barmen and Elberfeld, Engels made a similar report in 1839:[20]

The fresh, vigorous national life which is led almost everywhere in Germany eludes discovery here; at first sight this does not seem to be so, for every evening one can hear the merry fellows rolling along the streets, singing their songs, but these are the lowest obscene songs which have ever passed between brandy-soaked lips; never does one hear one of those folk-songs which are known all over the rest of Germany and of which we may be justly proud. All bars are full to overflowing, especially on Saturday and Sunday, and in the evening at eleven o'clock at closing time the drunks flock out of them to sleep off their drunkenness, mostly in the ditches . . .

The reasons for this behaviour are plain to see. In the first place, factory work is largely responsible. To work in low rooms where people inhale more coal-smoke and dust than oxygen, and usually from the age of six onwards, is just what is needed to deprive them of all drive and zest for life. Those weavers who have single looms in their homes sit from morn till late at night, huddled over them, and they let their spinal cords rot in the heat of the stove. Those who are not ensnared by Mysticism fall into brandy-quaffing.

A weaving song of the period runs as follows:

> The mother's son thus drinks away
> His weaver's wages earned by day.

Such descriptions would remind historians of the first half of the eighteenth century, of Hogarth perhaps and *Gin Lane*, of the drunken orgies in the streets and alleyways of London, and they would ask 'What's the difference?'

Here is what an economic historian has said about this phenomenon:

Finally we must consider one more separate class: the London proletariat of ragamuffins and part-time rogues, and the petty bourgeoisie. Considering the unique size of the city, there is something odd about them. In many ways they reflect the terrors of an age during which the original overcrowding continued to play an important part, for it uprooted people's lives and at the same time produced a large number of small-time crooks. The daily[21] gin-orgies are part of this phenomenon – one recalls the brutally realistic picture by Hogarth, *Gin Lane*, – as also are the great debtors' prison at Newgate and the terror spread by the penalties: death, or transportation to the colonies (one is reminded of Defoe's description in *Moll Flanders*). To this

Hogarth's *Gin Lane*, 1751.

same phenomenon belong the very high mortality rate among new-born babies of this class, and the correspondingly high percentage of children sold or handed over for work in mills or on the land. This class is heavily weighed down by the insecurity of existence and the gruesome barbarity of life, which the original period of overcrowding brought to all such people. It uprooted them and it utilised them, even in their uprooted condition, for its own ends, whether as consumers of gin made from corn, as forced labourers in the colonies, or even as whores or gangsters battling against capitalist competitors.[22]

This means that at that time, in the first half of the eighteenth century, the people who held such alcoholic orgies were not concerned in the processes of production, whereas in the first half of the nineteenth century the parties were held by the main body of workers in the most progressive and technically-advanced industry in the world. And as the factory proletariat at that time consisted mainly of women and children, they too became victims of alcoholism. This form of alcoholism was not primarily a cheerful vice, as it was perhaps among the Indians when they were first introduced to drinking 'fire', but to all intents and purposes a necessary moral stimulus. This is how it was described by a politician, later to be known far and wide, and a student of political economy, Moritz Mohl, in his early writings, when he was still Royal Assessor for Württemberg:

Who is going to condemn the spinner who works the whole week from five in the morning till ten at night if he goes off with his week's wages on Saturday evening, resolved to be a man for a day, having been a machine for six, lives in splendid style till Sunday evening, only to begin his day's work on Monday morning a beggar again, and to roll Sisyphus' stone once more up the mountain until the following Saturday?[23]

Who can wonder that illiteracy and ignorance in these circumstances were far more widespread than in the days of their fathers and grandfathers, when they in their turn were artisans or workers in domestic industry?

When we further consider that in this epoch, in comparison with the next, the percentage of skilled men among manual workers constantly declined, for it was the 'ingenious trick' of the machine that it could employ unskilled workers in ever increasing numbers; only then shall we realise that even the development of technical methods favoured the retention and spread of illiteracy and general ignorance.

So what has been written about these conditions seems to us to be borne out when we read in a report on a church and school inspection that

in our opinion the situation that has emerged from our official discussions, namely, that it is a usual practice to employ even children under ten years old in the factories on normal working days from five in the morning until eight in the evening, continuously, except for only the noon break and school hours, is a most unwholesome state of affairs, whose abolition seems all the more urgent and desirable in that children of such a tender age cannot fail to be so tired and worn out by this unremitting labour, that the hours spent in school instruction are, in my opinion as superintendent to be considered as good as wasted.[24]

In this instance we are dealing with a relatively civilised state of affairs, for the children referred to went to one of the schools attached to the factory, even if they were incapable of following the lessons through being exhausted by their factory work. In addition, instruction was given at a time in the day when they were no longer in a fit state to give of their best in factory production. In fact one would be quite justified in thinking that one of the chief advantages of these schools attached to factories was that they gave the children an opportunity of recovering from their labour in the factory, either by sleeping or dozing vacantly.

A large number of children however did not go to school at all. According to an investigation into educational conditions in Pendleton, near Manchester, it transpired that, of 2,657 children who in 1838 should have been going to school in this district, less than half, only 1,276, actually went to school at all regularly. But of those that did go to school, one third attended for less than three years. It was said about those who attended school that the 'schooling of a large proportion is attended with little or no practical

Sunday School, from Frances Trollope's
The Life and Adventures of Michael Armstrong, 1840.

benefit from the imperfect nature of such an education and the subsequent neglect which causes their slender acquirements to be soon forgotten.'

In the same account it was further noted 'that this [i.e. the forgetting of slender acquirements] would be the case to a much greater extent, were it not for Sunday schools.' And we should add that one quarter of a total of 4,512 people under the age of twenty-one had never, not even on an irregular basis, been to school; and three hundred and fifty had only attended Sunday school. Of the 1,287 under twenty-one who were attending school at the time of the investigation, 177 were under five years old, and were therefore sent there only so as not to remain unsupervised at home, because the adults were working, and naturally disturbed the lessons. Of the 4,512 under the age of twenty-one who were tested, 2,017 could not read, even though almost half their number were attending or had attended school! In addition to these there were a further 601 who were said to be 'barely able to read'. One has an even better idea of the poor schooling from the figures which follow: of 367 children who had had between two and three years training, only 144 could read, 131 could 'barely read' and ninety-two could not read at all.[25]

The situation elsewhere was similar to that in England and Germany. In France only little more than half the number of parishes – twenty-four thousand out of thirty-nine thousand – maintained even one school, and the number of illiterates was put at more than half the population.[26] Official statistics kept since 1832 on illiteracy among married couples reveal a total of fifty-three per cent illiterate during this year.

In the United States the *Mechanics' Magazine* of August 1833 (Vol II, No 69) puts the number of children between five and fifteen then attending school at one million. The *People's Magazine* gives the number for 1834 (in the issue dated 9 April 1834) as 1,250,000.

In any analysis of school conditions, one should not forget that there were several people within the ruling classes who considered literacy among the population to be a dangerous development. There was often the bitterest opposition to any progress in the realm of education. Giddy, a Member of Parliament and President of the Royal Society, argued as follows:

However specious in theory the project might be, of giving education to the labouring classes of the poor, it would in effect be found to be prejudicial to their morals and happiness; it would teach them to despise their lot in life, instead of making them good servants in agriculture, and other laborious employments to which their rank in society had destined them; instead of teaching them subordination, it would render them factious and refractory, as was evident in the manufacturing counties; it would enable them to read seditious pamphlets, vicious books, and publications against Christianity; it would render them insolent to their superiors; and in a few years the result would be that the legislature would find it necessary to direct the strong arm of power towards them, and to furnish the executive magistrate with much more vigorous laws than were now in force.[27]

With this in mind, Hobhouse has described a school started by a great landowner. It was intended for children of several parishes, but only forty children had places, the only ones who were allowed to attend by the landowner. All these children were to be taught to read, but only a small proportion of the forty – once again, it was the landowner's decision – were allowed to take part in the 'dangerous art' of writing and calculation.[28]

The beginnings of organisation

These circumstances caused millions to vegetate and their pointless existence was only occasionally interrupted with orgies enlivened by alcohol. It is all the more astonishing that groups of workers formed everywhere at this time. They were extremely active intellectually, they were filled with profound thoughts about the society in which they lived; and they had a crusading urge to change the life of the class which they represented.

Here is another example by Gorki: a description of factory workers on a festival day:

In the evening they strolled along the streets. Those who owned rubbers put them on even though the ground was dry, and those who owned umbrellas carried them even though the weather was fine.

On meeting their friends they spoke of the factory and of the machines and complained of the foreman: they thought and spoke only of things connected with their work. Occasionally the isolated sparks of faltering impotent thoughts penetrated the dull monotony of their days. When the men came home, they wrangled with their wives, and frequently beat them, unsparing of their own fists. The young people frequented the saloons or had parties at each others' houses where they played the accordion, sang coarse ugly songs, danced, swore and got drunk. Worn out as they were the liquor quickly went to their heads while a morbid incomprehensible irritation rankled in their breasts, demanding some outlet. For that reason they seized at the least opportunity to relieve their feelings, hurling themselves at each other with bestial ferocity on the slightest provocation. Bloody fights were the result. Sometimes they ended in serious injuries and occasionally in killings. A feeling of malice dominated their human relations and this feeling was as old as the incurable weariness of their muscles. People were born with this malady of the spirit inherited from their fathers and like a dark shadow it accompanied them to the very grave, causing them to perpetrate deeds revolting in their senseless cruelty. . . . After some fifty years of such a life a man died.[29]

So reads the introduction to the novel *Mother*, a novel whose main message is this: a thousand children may go to the factory in order to spend their lives there, like their parents, on the unchanging road between the cradle and the grave. One day a spark is born and it will join with other sparks which ignite in other places, to make one great fire. Men will tend the fire, they will spread it with constancy of purpose and will suffer endless sacrifices. They are the torch-bearers who are to light the way out of the conditions that have been described; well organised, together in close alliance – even if this is continually shattered – they will lead men out of misery.

The cultural, scientific, artistic and political achievements of the ruling classes are wonderful. One recalls the slave-owners of Greece, the feudal lords and the bourgeoisie of past times. Only on the basis of these achievements could these men lead and control a new society.

Never in history have the oppressed classes been able to produce significant cultural achievements in larger quantities. Friedrich Engels expressed it in these words:

So long as the real working population is so much engaged in its essential work, that it has no time available to see to the normal activities of society: control of labour, government business, legal matters, art, science, etc.; then a special class will continue to be necessary, free from real work and thereby enabled to see to these affairs; in doing so they have never failed to unload on to the labouring masses an ever-growing burden of work, to their own advantage.[30]

The working class, about whose emergence this book is being written, was the first class of those manually employed in production, fundamentally differing from all its predecessors in history, in that its products were of universal importance to civilisation. This opportunity was given to them – and Hegel would call it a 'trick of history' – by the machine; the machine, which alienated them from their work. from their working life, made them into its appendages, appropriated and annexed their intellectual life. Engels explained it in this way:

It is obvious that, so long as human labour continued to be so unproductive that it produced only a small surplus over and above essential supplies, an increase in productive power, extension of trade, development of the state and the law, the founding of art and science were only made possible by an increased distribution of work, which had to have as its basis the great division of work between the masses who carried out simple hand-work, and those few who were privileged to control labour, trade and public affairs, and later occupied themselves with art and science. . . . It was only the enormous increase in productive power attained by large-scale industry which allowed work to be distributed among all members of society without exception and thus enabled everyone's working hours to be so limited that sufficient free time remained for all to take part in the normal activities of society, both theoretical and practical.[31]

It was the machine which made possible such high productivity of work. It was also the machine that led to an increasing intensity of labour. And it was this increasing intensity of labour which forced the employer, objectively and for physiological reasons, to shorten the hours of work and give in to the workers who were fighting for these shorter working hours. The combination of physiological reasons and the battles of the workers led to shorter working hours at the end of the period under considerations, and thereby gave the working class the opportunity to begin its great rôle in society.

There are many factors which determine the workers' mode of life: real wages, working hours, living and sanitary conditions, their constitutional status (right to vote, combination rights, etc.), accident benefit, social insurance, and more besides. Yet one factor was of decisive importance for the period under discussion and for the future: the extent of working hours. It stands to reason that men who work a daily minimum of thirteen and a maximum of eighteen hours, inclusive of breaks at work, travelling time and working time, have neither the time nor the physical nor mental energy to organise themselves on a political or industrial basis, to educate themselves, to stump up and down the country, to spread propaganda: in other words, to busy themselves with social life in a way other than by manual toil.

But, as has already been observed, the period when working hours were reduced falls outside our present investigation. In England the ten-hour bill was adopted in 1847, not least as a result of the impression caused by Macaulay's speech, in which he took up the cudgels against the opponents of the shorter working day with these words:

They reason thus. We cannot reduce the number of hours of labour in factories without reducing the amount of production. We cannot reduce the amount of production without reducing the remuneration of the labourer. Meanwhile, foreigners, who are at liberty to work until they drop down dead at their looms, will soon beat us out of all the markets of the world. Wages will go down fast. The condition of our working people will be far worse than it is; and our unwise interference will, like the unwise interference of our ancestors with the dealings of the corn factor and the money lenders, increase the distress of the very class which we wish to relieve. . . .

Sir, exactly three hundred years ago, great religious changes were taking place in England. Much was said and written, in that inquiring and inno- vating age, about the question whether Christians were under a religious obligation to rest from labour on one day in the week; and it is well known that the chief Reformers, both here and on the continent, denied the exis- tence of any such obligation. Suppose then that, in 1546, Parliament had made a law that there should thenceforth be no distinction between the Sunday and any other day. Now, Sir, our opponents, if they are consistent with themselves, must hold that such a law would have immensely increased the wealth of the country and the remuneration of the working man. What an effect, if their principles be sound, must have been produced by the addition of one sixth to the time of labour! What an increase of production! What a rise of wages! How utterly unable must the foreign artisan, who still had his days of festivity and of repose, have found himself to maintain a competition with a people whose shops were open, whose markets were crowded, whose spades, and axes, and planes, and hods, and anvils, and looms were at work from morning till night on three hundred and sixty-five days a year! The Sundays of three hundred years make up fifty years of our working days. We know what the industry of fifty years can do. We know what marvels the industry of the last fifty years has wrought. The arguments of my honourable friend irresistibly lead us to this conclusion, that if, during the last three centuries, the Sunday had not been observed as a day of rest, we should have been far better off than at present. But does he, does any Member of the House, seriously believe that this would have been the case? For my own part, I have not the smallest doubt that, if we and our ancestors had, during the last three centuries, worked just as hard on the Sundays as on the week days, we should have been at this moment a poorer people and a less civilised people than we are; that there would have been less production than there has been, that the wages of the labourer would have been lower than they are, and that some other nation would have been now making cotton stuffs and woollen stuffs and cutlery for the whole world.[32]

In France, the reduction of working hours began with the revolution of 1848; in Belgium and Holland at about the same time, in Germany somewhat later, and still later in Italy and Austria.

It can certainly be said that since the eighteen-fifties the struggle for the reduction of working hours gained more and more in importance. Thus for example in Germany the following were the percentages of all strikes which were to do with working hours, whether separately or in conjunction with wages:

1850–57	7·6 per cent
1858–66	13·0 per cent
1867–70	17·6 per cent

In the United States, the struggle for the reduction of working hours was waged by the engineers' and smiths' trade union at an annual congress in Boston in 1863, with the following declaration of the main objective of the labour movement:

Resolved, that from east to west, from north to south, the most important change to us as working men, to which all else is subordinate, is a permanent reduction to eight of the hours exacted for each day's work . . .

Resolved, that a reduction of hours is an increase of wages . . . .

Resolved, that a reduction of the number of hours for a day's work, be the cardinal point to which our movement ought to be directed; that we make this point with the understanding that it is not antagonistic with capital, while at the same time it invests our cause with the dignity and power of a great moral and social reform, and that it is every way worthy of the sympathy and co-operation of the most progressive and liberal thinkers of the age, and that the time has fully arrived in which to commence a thorough and systematic agitation of this, the leading point in the great problem of labor reform.[33]

Thus the question of working hours was to be the one on which the whole energies of the labour movement had to concentrate. By a shortening of the working day, the unions believed that they could abolish all the ills which the workers endured. They believed in the possibility of raising the workers' standard of living by reducing working hours, and they also believed that this would not militate against the interests of the employer.

What process of thought lay at the root of this argument?

In his pamphlet *A reduction of hours, an increase of wages*, Ira Steward argues as follows[34]:

Those who have to work hardest and longest receive the lowest wages, while those whose work is more attractive earn more, as a general rule, and many who do absolutely nothing earn still more. One may thus conclude that those who work hardest and longest receive their low wages precisely because their work is so long and hard. Those who work too hard are so worn out and exhausted that they desire to do nothing but satisfy their physical needs; on the other hand, those who work less have the time to cultivate their tastes and they have desires which go beyond purely material needs. Those who work so hard and for so long cannot be induced to demand higher wages, because they have no strength left, no time and no desire. Think of a man who works fourteen hours a day; he has no time to have a bath, write letters, grow flowers, have guests or look at works of art. For him his dwelling-place means eating and sleeping. On the other hand, a man who works only eight hours per day has much more time at his disposal.

In Steward's own words:

My theory is:

First, that more leisure will create motives and temptations for the common people to ask for more wages.

Second, that where all ask for more wages, there will be no motive for refusing, since employers will all fare alike.

Third, that where all demand more wages, the demand cannot be resisted.

Fourth, that resistance would amount to the folly of a 'strike' by employers themselves, against the strongest power in the world, viz. the habits, customs, and opinions, of the masses.

Fifth, that the change in the habits and opinions of the people through more leisure will be too gradual to disturb or jar the commerce and enterprise of capital.

Sixth, that the increase in wages will fall upon the wastes of society, in its crimes, idleness, fashions, and monopolies, as well as the more legitimate and honorable profits of capital, in the production and distribution of wealth, and

Seventh, in the mechanical fact that the cost of making an article depends almost entirely upon the number manufactured is a practical increase of wages, by tempting the workers, through their new leisure, to unite in buying luxuries now confined to the wealthy, and which are costly because bought only by the wealthy.[35]

In connection with point number seven, Steward also expected that a shortened working day should eliminate the 'capitalistic corruption by the control of literature, of politics and of the national daily press'. For with the reduced working hours, the workers' demand for literature would grow enormously, and authors would no longer be dependent on the employer's wishes.

In 1863 a theory of this kind was born in the United States. Naturally, however, there is a gap between conception and birth, which in the world of ideas is very large. And further, a working class which is aware of the political and cultural significance of the reduction of working hours, and which, as soon as it comes on the scene, makes use of them to the same extent as the class which was born during the Industrial Revolution, must already have within it the germ of its rôle in society, and begin to develop it, particularly if this class had, up to 1850, such outstanding helpers from the bourgeoisie and petty bourgeoisie as the radicals and utopians and above all, Marx and Engels.

If we except the slaves of antiquity who frequently came from all corners of the earth and then could not understand one another's language, people working with their hands have always been organised in one way or another. But they were always divided for practical reasons by their position within society, and had completely different objectives.

It is otherwise under capitalism, which creates for itself an army of a million manual workers in the same social position, and they have the same interests.

Sée, in his work on the origins of modern capitalism, notes:

The effect of capitalist wholesale manufacture in France, as in England, was to create an often unbridgeable chasm between employers and employees. Hence the working class would become more clearly aware of their common interests, which would have been impossible for them in the days when masters and journeymen had led almost the same kind of life, and there had not been such a sharp division between the different industrial classes. Workers were to organise themselves in defence of their class interests, and much earlier in England than in France, because there this evolution had taken place at a much earlier date and had affected far greater numbers of the common people. Now it was no longer, as in 1789, the peasant question, but the worker question which claimed attention.[36]

Naturally the factory workers were not the first to form their trade-unions and friendly societies. One should read what Hutt has to say, for example, about the early English unions:

By the end of the eighteenth century trade unions had begun to take root, in the shape of local trade clubs which usually met in public-houses and bore a marked social character (liquor was an important item in the official expenditure). For the most part, these trade clubs had developed among the artisan 'aristocracy', the skilled handicraftsmen whose methods of work and conditions the Industrial Revolution had yet left substantially untouched; the compositors, coopers, carpenters and joiners, cabinet-makers, shipwrights, papermakers, and so forth.

These organisations had nothing yet to do with unions of the industrial working class. Nevertheless, these are Hutt's concluding remarks on this topic:

But from 1792 they had begun to spread among the key section of the new factory workers, the Lancashire cotton spinners; and this potential threat to the rising capitalist employers, coupled with the panic induced among the ruling class by the French Revolution set the stage for the hurried passage through Parliament in 1799–1800 of the notorious Combination Acts.[37]

There were certainly great differences between these two sorts of organisation. The important point is that the Combination Acts passed in 1799 and then, in a slightly more moderate form thanks to the opposition led by the famous playwright Sheridan, in 1800 were directed much more harshly against factory workers than against artisans, domestic weavers, and others. It is therefore understandable that William Lovett, a rope-maker and joiner, found it possible to say in his autobiography that, when he came to London during the currency of the Combination Acts, he had been unable to find any work in his trade without becoming a member of a trade union. The Webbs assessed the matter thus:

In place of the steady organised resistance to encroachments maintained by the handicraftsmen, we watch, in the machine industries, the alternation of outbursts of machine-breaking and outrages, with intervals of abject submission and reckless competition with each other for employment. In the conduct of such organisation as there was, repressive laws had, with the operatives as with the London artisans, the effect of throwing great power into the hands of a few men. These leaders were implicitly obeyed in times of industrial conflict, but the repeated defeats which they were unable to avert prevented that growth of confidence which is indispensable for permanent organisation.[38]

Thus Engels remarks, perhaps somewhat pessimistically:

The story of these combinations is a long succession of workers' defeats punctuated by a few isolated victories.[39]

And it was not only that the organisation among workers in factories was much more difficult, for they came from so many different levels and were often nothing but casual labour, or at least thought they were. In addition, the principal cause of the almost insuperable difficulties was that personnel consisted so largely of women and children. And yet, we have only to look at the situation in New England at a time when the majority of industrial workers were women and children. Women took part in many strikes; and the first one was probably that of the weavers in Pawtucket, Rhode Island, in 1824. Many strikes were even conducted almost exclusively by women, as occasionally there were trade unions and other similar organisations to which only women belonged; for example, the *Female Society of Lynn and Vicinity for the Protection and Promotion of Female Industry* or the one founded a few years later (1845 or 1847) and led by Sarah G. Bagley, *Lowell Female Reform Association*. (There were also special pamphlets written about female working hours such as *The Factory Girl* in New Hampshire (1842). In support of the women, children stood resolutely on strike pickets, and in one case a strike-breaker, prevented from working by children, brought a court action against them.

In a worker's reminiscences there is a passage about a strike in which women were the principal participants:

One of the first strikes that ever took place in this country was in Lowell in 1836. When it was announced that the wages were to be cut down, great indignation was felt, and it was decided to strike or 'turn out' *en masse*. This was done. The mills were shut down, and the girls went from their several corporations in procession to the grove on Chapel Hill, and listened to incendiary speeches from some early labor reformers. One of the girls stood on a pump and gave vent to the feelings of her companions in a neat speech, declaring that it was their duty to resist all attempts at cutting down the wages. This was the first time a woman had spoken in public in Lowell, and the event caused surprise and consternation among her audience. One of the number, a little girl eleven years old, had led the turn-out from the room in which she worked.[40]

In the U.S.A. there was no official law, as in England, which forbade trade unions; but in practice, legal pronouncements often reduced to naught any possibility of their having any effect. However, between 1806 and 1815, the shoemakers of Philadelphia, New York, Baltimore and Pittsburg, were six times arraigned and sentenced for 'criminal conspiracy'. Under the pressure from the masses (the following years saw the election of progressive judges in Philadelphia and New York) the right to organise trade unions was granted in the North, but without simultaneous or general recognition by the courts that important trade union activities, such as the posting of strike pickets, strikes and boycotts were legal weapons of the labour movement. Even in 1831 a workman's book carried the complaint 'If mechanics combine to raise their wages, the laws punish them. ... But the laws have made it a just and meritorious act that capitalists shall combine to strip the man of labour of his earnings.'[41]

To some extent, children in industry were subject to special laws, particularly if they were apprentices. The strike of calico-printers in Chemnitz in 1823, for example, collapsed not least because both factory owners and apprentice masters told the apprentices that their indentures would become null and void if they took part in the strike, and the town council threatened them with imprisonment if they did not work. As the apprentices comprised about fifteen per cent of the workers, they were extremely important people.[42]

In the early period of the labour movement, especially, it is difficult to distinguish between economic and political organisations, such as trade unions and parties. Trade unions of course always have a certain number of political aims, and parties without an economic programme are unthinkable. On the other hand, after 1850, it was certainly possible to differentiate between trade unions which had no separate political ideology peculiar to the workers, and parties which were imbued with political ideologies of a superior kind. But before that date, when the different types of organisation were not yet distinctly drawn, it was indeed difficult.

There is in addition the extraordinary variety of motives for ideologies in which the only common features were often hatred of the present and the desire to create a better future here on earth by active means and by one's own energies. This has been very well illustrated by Hobsbawm, even though he has omitted to emphasise the significance of the separate ideologies:

The labour movement was an organisation of self-defence, of protest, of revolution. But for the labouring poor it was more than a tool of struggle: it was also a way of life. The liberal bourgeoisie offered them nothing; history took them away from the traditional life which conservatives offered vainly to maintain or to restore. Neither had much to do with the sort of life into which they were increasingly drawn. But the movement had, or rather, the way of life which they hammered out for themselves, collective, communal, combative, idealist, and isolated, implied the movement, for struggle was its very essence. And in return the movement gave it coherence and purpose. The liberal myth supposed that unions were composed of feckless labourers instigated by conscienceless agitators, but in reality the feckless were generally the least unionised, the most intelligent and competent workers, the most firm in their support for union.

The most highly developed examples of such 'worlds of labour' in this period were probably still those of the old domestic industries. There was

Trade union protest meeting
at Copenhagen Field, 1834,
against the deportation of
the Tolpuddle Martyrs.

the community of the Lyon silk-workers, the ever-rebellious *canuts* – who rose in 1831 and again in 1834, and who in Michelet's phrase, 'because this world would not do, made themselves another in the humid obscurity of their alleys, a moral paradise of sweet dreams and visions.' There were communities such as those of the Scottish linen-weavers with their republican and Jacobin puritanism, their Swedenborgian heresies, their Tradesmen's Library, savings' bank, Mechanics' Institute, Library and Scientific Club, their Drawing Academy, missionary meetings, temperance leagues, and infant schools, their Florists' Society and literary magazine (the *Dunfermline Gasometer*) – and of course their Chartism. Class-consciousness, militancy, hatred and contempt for the oppressor, belonged to this life as much as the looms on which men wove. They owed nothing to the rich except their wages. What they had in life was their own collective creation.

But this silent process of self-organisation was not confined to workers of this older type. It is reflected in the 'union', often based on the local Primitive Methodist community, in the Northumberland and Durham mines. It is reflected in the dense concentration of workers' mutual and friendly societies in the new industrial areas, especially Lancashire. Above all, it is reflected in the serried thousands of men, women and children who streamed with torches on to the moors for Chartist demonstrations from the smaller industrial towns of Lancashire, in the rapidity with which the new Rochdale co-operative shops spread in the latter eighteen-forties.[43]

The labour movement in England was of course the most comprehensive. There were movements which continued for years like that of the Chartists, which included revolutionaries and reformers, and sent a petition to Parliament with a million signatures for a reform of the franchise, and which also decided on a general strike at their convention on 5 August 1839:

That from the evidence which has reached this council from the various parts of the country, we are unanimously of opinion that the people are not prepared to carry out the sacred month on the 12th August. The same evidence however convinces us that the great body of the working people including most of the trades may be induced to cease work on the 12th instant, for one, two or three days, in order to devote the whole of that time to solemn processions and meetings, for deliberating on the present awful state of the country, and devising the best means of averting the hideous despotism, with which the industrious orders are menaced by the murderous majority of the upper and middle classes who prey upon their labour.[44]

There were no such movements yet in other countries.

On the other hand, labour movements of explosive bitterness, such as in France – which, as in 1830, had a considerable rôle in the Revolution and (cf. June 1848) set their seal on it – are not to be found in other countries.

In comparison with France and England, the labour movement in Germany lagged very far behind. Engels stated in his essay on the history of the League of Communists, when discussing the situation at the end of the period we are discussing:

In those days one had to choose workers separately who were able to understand their condition as workers and their historical and economic antagonism to capital, because this antagonism itself was just beginning to be comprehended.[45]

In the United States the political labour movement, as in Germany, was extraordinarily weak; not least because the class boundaries were still so much easier to cross and democracy was much more intensively developed than in Europe; whereas a not unimportant part began to be played by trade union organisations of local and national character, national within the professions and indeed in all trades.

Now all these organisations were built up by people who rarely had more, and often less, than the bare necessities of life, who worked the whole day long, from sunrise to sunset, and frequently for much longer in winter. Every hour of agitation and propaganda deprived them of an hour of sleep, which was anyway insufficient, and they were threatened by the supreme power of the state, the local authorities and the tyranny of their factory masters or owners, with imprisonment or hard labour, the loss of their job and the refusal of work from any other employer; or with transportation to the colonies!

Many of these early heroes and martyrs of the labour movement

Robert Owen, 1771–1858. As a successful mill-owner, he introduced better labouring conditions and housing for the workers and better schooling for local children, and was a pioneer of adult education. He developed a new social order based on cooperation rather than competition, which attracted attention on the Continent and in the United States. Even after practical experiments failed, he still believed in the immediate overthrow of capitalism and the introduction of the 'new moral order'.

were illiterate politicians and philosophers of considerable importance. Others were autodidacts of wide education; and they were joined by representatives from other grades and classes: Robert Owen, originally perhaps the craftiest and most able profiteer of his time; Charles Fourier, wealthy heir of a merchant family; Friedrich Engels, son of an equally pious and well-to-do factory owner's family; or even Francis Place, an opulent master-tailor; Horace Greeley, the successful newspaper publisher; Auguste Blanqui, a former tutor; and Karl Marx, son of a patriotic Prussian lawyer.

Working-class culture

A class wishing to establish itself under capitalism needed a fundamentally different kind of culture from that required under feudalism. If the most important problems of human life were disguised in religious terms in the former age, if in those days it was impossible to imagine any advancement for the 'little man' other than by religious reasoning; then capitalism, which divested itself of so many of its disguises, brought pure knowledge to the point of almost mystical importance. 'Knowledge is power', that aphorism of the great Bacon, who wanted to found a logical science of discovery, became the battle-cry of the working class.

When the distinguished German publisher Joseph Meyer started a penny-library of German classics in 1848, he considered them, as he put it, to be 'a tool for the intellectual emancipation of the masses'.

All 'friends of the workers' and the workers themselves were united. Those who wanted to 'draw the workers to them' were in agreement. Also those who watched for the time when workers would gain their freedom as a separate class in the fight against capital; all were agreed that education and knowledge were of decisive importance.

It is difficult to comprehend what this means in the story of humanity. One must bear in mind that before capitalism not a single ruling class considered it necessary even for its own members to be able to read and write. There were of course slave-owners, in addition to feudal lords, who could read and write, and naturally they kept such people as could do so to themselves. But even as illiterates they managed to fulfil their historical functions. Not so the bourgeoisie; certainly not capital.

And now an oppressed class was demanding to be able to read and write!

There was, of course, opposition at first, and there were 'taxes on knowledge', as bourgeois radicals in England used to call them. The bourgeoisie took Bacon seriously and with some justification: knowledge is power, or, as they conveniently turned it: without knowledge no power.

How successful such taxes on knowledge could be can be seen in just one example. The greatest political agitator in England, William Cobbett, published a sort of newspaper in the first thirty years of the century called the *Political Register*, directed ideologically towards the working population, though it could scarcely be bought by them as it cost one shilling and a halfpenny, including taxes. But when in 1816 a special number containing no news and therefore not liable for tax was issued for twopence, over two hundred thousand copies were printed.

But now all countries contained true champions of the working

A PETERLOO MEDAL.

Q. " Am I not a man and a brother?"
A. " No!—you are a poor weaver!"

class, who stood up for freedom of speech, cheap printing-costs
and the spread of knowledge. One of the great men in this struggle
was Richard Carlile, who owned a bookshop and had to spend
nine and a half years in various prisons before he won a partial
victory. This was a struggle in which his wife took part, but she
too was put in prison in spite of her pregnancy; her sister, who took
the condemned woman's place, and a whole army of volunteer
shop-assistants, also took part, and they were sentenced to a total
of between one hundred and fifty and two hundred years' imprisonment; or at least until the revocation, in 1817, of the law forbidding
the sale of 'slanderous' writings, 'dangerous to the state'.

A Peterloo medal, from the satirical pamphlet
A Slap at Slop, 1821. In 1819 there was
a meeting at St Peter's Field, Manchester,
of some 60,000 people demanding parliamentary reform.
This peaceable meeting was charged by hussars and the
yeomanry, and at least 600 people were killed.

One of Carlile's volunteer shop assistants left memoirs from which it is worth quoting, if only to know what these 'slanderous' writings, 'dangerous to the state' were:

It was in the autumn of 1818 that I first became acquainted with politics and theology. Passing along Briggate one evening, I saw ... a bill which stated that the Radical Reformers held their meetings in a room in that court. Curiosity prompted me to go and hear what was going on. I found them reading Wooler's *Black Dwarf*, Carlile's *Republican* and Cobbett's *Register*. I remembered my mother being in the habit of reading Cobbett's *Register* and saying she wondered people spoke so much against it; she saw nothing bad in it! After hearing it read in the meeting room I was of my mother's opinion.

From this time until 1822 I was actively engaged in collecting subscriptions for Mr Carlile, spreading the liberal and free-thinking literature and by meetings and discussions endeavouring to obtain the right of free discussion. In 1821 the government renewed the prosecutions for blasphemy and Mr Carlile (then in Dorchester gaol) appealed to the friends in the country to serve in the shop. ... On 1st September 1822 I arrived in London. ... I served in the shop at 5, Water Lane, Fleet Street. At this time the plan of selling the books by a sort of clockwork so that the seller was not seen was in practice. ... Towards the end of February I was arrested for selling a copy of Palmer's *Principles of Nature*. Sent to Clerkenwell Prison where I remained six weeks ... my trial took place on the 23rd April. ... I was convicted and sentenced to twelve months' imprisonment in Coldbath-Field's prison and to find bail for my good behaviour for two years ... I endeavoured to make the best use of the opportunity for study and investigation. I was liberated on 24th April.[46]

Side by side with these brave champions of working-class interests was an important group within the middle class, whose aim was both objective, in their own interests, and subjective, in that they were often filled with humane feelings of friendliness towards the workers; namely, to help the workers to gain knowledge in order to turn them into a petty bourgeoisie, fully integrated in society, and to make them into voters for the Conservatives or Liberals in order to give the group political identity. This was an undertaking in which astonishingly enough they succeeded in

130

England in the second half of the nineteenth century. But it did not succeed in Germany where similar efforts were made; nor in France.

This was an attitude of paternalism in sharp contrast to the attitude of those who wanted no benevolent fathers for the working class, but wished to be independent. Not infrequently these two groups clashed within the same institutions. The best-known example of this sort of clash were the battles over the so-called 'mechanics' or 'working-men's' institutes in England. The latter, round seven hundred in about 1850, could boast of over one hundred thousand members and over seven hundred thousand books in their libraries. However, a third factor was involved in the problems of these institutes, particularly in the early days of their foundation, a factor which is of high sociological interest. These institutes aimed to make skilled workmen into inventors, masters of science, who, like their grandfathers at the beginning of the Industrial Revolution, were to advance technical progress, and help the continued development of the forces of production as if there were really no classes at all. The wild passion for profitable development of the forces of production, the unfamiliarity of dealing with impersonal class barriers, were possibly the original motives which caused the bourgeoisie to set up these institutes. The first institute to be set up was a Mechanics Institute in London in 1823. Others quickly followed. In 1825 in the West Riding alone there were institutes at Bradford, Keighley, Wakefield, Dewsbury, Halifax, Huddersfield, Skipton and Richmond.[4] Instruction was given for the most part in the realms of natural sciences: in chemistry, physics, mathematics, 'mechanics', and so on. The aims of these institutions were defined as follows: they would 'send hundreds, nay thousands, of a new set of labourers into the boundless and half-cultivated fields of science; to explore new tracts, find new riches, and add to the heap of existing knowledge.'[48] 'A new race of philosophers' was to arise, as the speaker put it.

Marx observed, with Ricardo, that in his completely honest

efforts to develop the forces of production, he even occasionally gave up his class point of view. In the same way an entire movement was in theory, in their plans and in the practical instruction being given, straying briefly over the class boundaries, at the last possible moment before the political breach opened at the time of the clash on fundamentals between capital and labour in 1832. It was a rare phenomenon, which has been insufficiently studied for its odd features. Yet one must not forget in this early period of the Mechanics Institute that the founders in London were left-wing radicals like Hodgskin, Gast and others, though it was soon penetrated by utilitarians. In the battle of the institute, the study plan played a decisive part; the workers insisted on 'their' economy (that of Hodgskin, Owen, and so on), the utilitarians on theirs (the bourgeoisie's). The compromise which resulted was that political economy was not taught at all.

In 1849 these institutes were almost all in the hands of the middle class even when so many battles were going on and the workers were trying to back out of bourgeois tutelage. In Nottingham, for instance, in 1849, they gradually left the institute and formed their own 'workers' library'.[49]

Nevertheless, whoever was in control of these institutes, one thing should never be forgotten. The attitude of the greater part of society towards the education of the workers was expressed exactly by a progressive clergyman, Robertson, when he declared:

There was still among a very poor population [in Winchester] of from three to four thousand, much infidelity and immorality—the children of a long neglect. Violent opposition was made to the building of a new church, and still more violent to the establishment of parochial schools, not only by a number of small shopkeepers, who were bitterly prejudiced and ignorant, but also by the old High Church gentry of the parish, who looked upon schools as dangerous innovations.[50]

At the end of the period under consideration, in February 1848, appeared the *Communist Manifesto*. At that time it was published by one of the many hundreds of (international) workers' political movements, called the *Communist League* – a daughter of the *League of the Just*, and grand-daughter of the *League of Outlaws* – a union of Germans, French, Englishmen, Swiss, Belgians, Scandinavians, Dutchmen, Hungarians, Czechs, Russians, South Slavs and others. Such international leagues did not yet represent the union of mature, important national movements at an international level; they were just the opposite, an indication of the immaturity of the labour movement. For their mainstays were not the industrial proletariat, but wandering craft journeymen, particularly tailors, but in addition shoemakers, clockmakers, joiners, carpenters and also a few intellectuals like Engels and Marx.

The *Communist Manifesto* nonetheless spoke for the working class, and in particular for the industrial proletariat. It declared war, not on the employers of this league's members, so much as on the core of the ruling classes – capital. It summoned to the fight all the employed and oppressed, but principally the industrial proletariat. It is for that reason one of the most significant documents of human civilisation, because it combines a profound analysis of the great, historic movement of human beings (who value progress, whatever its source), with a passionate appeal for the destruction of the prevailing system.

Whatever its source, as Engels rightly said in the foreword to the Italian edition in 1893, 'the *Manifesto* metes justice out to the revolutionary part played by capitalism in the past.' And Edgar Salin who today, in Basle, is in fact a very conservative student of political economy, spoke forty years ago about the 'Hymn to the Bourgeoisie' in the *Communist Manifesto*. Who has ever depicted the achievements of the bourgeoisie so excellently, so deeply comprehended what it brought to mankind, or described it so strikingly? Here is an extract:

The bourgeoisie, by the rapid improvement of all instruments of production, by the constant easing of communications, draws all, even the most barbarian, nations into civilisation. The cheap prices of its goods are the heavy artillery with which it knocks down all Chinese walls, and with which it brings the most obstinate xenophobia of barbarians to its knees. It compels

134

The Communist Manifesto,
published in London,
February 1848.

all nations to adopt the production methods of the bourgeoisie, if they do not want to be ruined; it forces them to introduce their country to so-called civilisation themselves, that is to say, to become bourgeois. In a word, it creates a world after its own image.

The bourgeoisie has subjected the country to the hegemony of the town. It has created enormous cities, it has greatly increased the size of the urban population in comparison with the rural, and has thus rescued an appreciable section of the population from the idiocy of rural life. It has made the country dependent on the town, and likewise the wild and half-wild nations on the civilised, the peasants on the bourgeois, the East on the West.

The bourgeoisie continues to abolish scattered means of production, scattered ownership and scattered populations. It has grouped the population, centralised the means of production and concentrated property in the hands of the few. The inevitable consequence of this was political centralisation. Independent provinces in an almost loose federation, with different interests, laws, governments and tax-systems were compressed into one nation, one government, one law, one national class interest, one customs tariff.

The bourgeoisie has created in its rule of the upper classes, barely one hundred years old, more massive, more colossal forces of production than all previous generations put together. Harnessing of natural forces, machinery, utilisation of chemistry for industry and agriculture, steam-navigation, railways, electric telegraph, cultivation of vast tracts of the earth's surface, making rivers navigable, conjuring up whole populations out of the ground: what previous century dreamed that such productive forces slumbered in the lap of social toil?

And this in a manifesto whose world-famous concluding words were:

Communists scorn to keep secret their opinions and intentions. They declare openly that their aims can only be achieved by a forcible overthrow of all previous social contracts. Let the ruling classes tremble before a Communist revolution. Proletarians have nothing to lose but their shackles. They have a world to win. Proletarians of all lands, unite!

In this work the ideological maturity of the working class was of the highest order. In some ways it outstripped its own evolution. When the Communist League commissioned Marx and Engels in 1847 to sketch out a 'detailed theoretical and practical party programme', and when, at the beginning of 1848 it adopted the *Communist Manifesto*, no one suspected that exactly one hundred years later this work would be printed in an edition which outsold every other publication of that year. It even outsold the Bible which for centuries, practically since the beginning of book-printing in Europe, had been a best-seller.

So when the last century was completing one half of its span, the human race began a new epoch in its history: a new class had emerged and was already aware of its existence.

4 The rise of
the working class:
national differences

Anonymous French cartoon, 1789, depicting the advantages of the free Frenchman over the enslaved Englishman. Pitt is trampling on the crown and holding Parliament enchained.

In the foregoing pages, we have frequently used the words ' . . . and it was the same elsewhere: in England, France, the United States of America, Germany, Belgium and Italy'. This shows that, in the main, we have elaborated the common features in their development. In doing so, however, it was inevitable that here and there certain peculiarities had to be pointed out, albeit unwillingly, so as not to disturb the broad lines of the picture with too delicate brush-strokes.

In this chapter our aim is quite different. It is just these peculiarities in the development of industrial progress within the four main countries which are to be elaborated. At the same time, we shall not avoid pointing out common features from time to time, our reasons being pedagogic and for both the author's and the reader's benefit. For we must never forget the unity of the whole in studying the particular, not so much because this is so fundamentally important in the study of the rise of the working class, but more because it is indispensable in order to understand the developments which took place after the period here under consideration. Otherwise one cannot comprehend the full significance of the international political parties and trade unions as representative of what we call the universal proletariat.

In what order are we to take the countries, and why is it the peculiarities only of Germany, England, France and the United States which we are examining in detail?

We shall examine the development in England first; for England is justly considered to be the 'classical example'. Engels wrote as much in the foreword to his *Condition of the Working Classes in England*:

It is only in the British Empire, and particularly in England itself, that proletarian conditions exist in their classical and complete form.

And the aristocratic reviewer of the book said as much in the Prussian government newspaper already quoted:

England is, without any doubt, the country in which proletarian conditions have reached their highest point of development. From England we may learn what hazards a nation must avoid if it wants to achieve power and position without being exposed to the same evils and dangers as that country; the story of the English proletariat is for us the textbook of practical experience.

We shall make a direct comparison between England and the United States because conditions in the States were so different; one might even have doubted whether it was possible to refer to a working class there in about 1850, in spite of the very powerful development of industry; doubts which one certainly had in Australia, New Zealand and Canada in the eighteen-seventies. After that we shall turn to France, which offers such a strange contrast between the relative weaknesses of her economic, and the relative strength of her political, development. Finally we have to go further into what produced the conditions in Germany, which economically and politically lagged so far behind, that one could still describe it as a semi-feudal country even in the 1840s. Nor must one lose sight of the fact that the development in Germany was in many ways typical too for Austria and some other regions of Eastern Europe.

In considering these countries we have not only included by far the most important section of the working class, quantitatively speaking, which evolved between 1760 and 1850. We have also investigated the main lines of its development. Moreover, it must not be forgotten, as we shall be showing at the end of this investigation, that the later formation of working classes (under conditions of colonial rule in India, for example), naturally shows peculiarities which we do not find in the countries mentioned here.

England: the classical model

A working class evolved in England before all other countries, because it was in England that machines were first used in production. A study of conditions in England therefore poses the question why we have given the starting date as 1760 in this book about the rise of the working class.

The reasons for stating such a definite date must obviously be somewhat arbitrary, though, strangely enough, all kinds of scholars of the last century or more have agreed on this year. Engels names it[1] and so do Toynbee,[2] Mantoux,[3] the Hammonds,[4] and Fay[5]; as also does the Great Soviet Encyclopaedia in its history of England. Yet none of them gives a precise reason for the choice of this year. 1760 is in fact an arbitrarily chosen date in as much as the situation in that year compared with 1759 or 1761 showed scarcely any difference. But 1760 ushered in a new decade, in which the Industrial Revolution was definitely in full swing. Hargreaves was preparing the ground for his invention of the Spinning Jenny (completed in 1764), Watt was doing the same for his steam engine (completed in 1764), Brindley's canal between Worsley and Manchester was under construction in 1760, and Matthew Boulton's large factory in Soho, Birmingham was built. In addition, 1760 coincided with the zenith and collapse of the government of Chatham, England's most famous Prime Minister of the manufacturing era. These are the reasons for placing the beginning of the Industrial Revolution in the years round 1760.[6]

This means that the beginnings of a modern labour force in England, and therefore on a world scale, can be seen at the opening of the second decade of the second half of the eighteenth century: so the working class was born some two hundred years ago.

And as the machine – the forceps used by society to deliver the working class – was first introduced into the cotton industry, the first modern proletariat in the world was in the cotton industry. It is therefore quite natural for David Landes to begin his chapter on the technical and industrial development of Western Europe between 1750 and 1914 in the *Cambridge Economic History*[7] with two numbers: the year 1760, and a raw cotton import by England amounting, in that year, to two and a half million pounds. Referring to the cotton industry of that year, he says that it was mainly centred in the countryside round Lancashire and could only exist in close co-operation with the linen industry, as only the latter was capable of supplying the warp-yarn the other required. At that

A Yorkshire collier, 1813. Only
in England at this date was the
miner a member of a working
class already in its second or
third generation.

time the working class, as we have seen, was born in England, and being a 'child of the country' it was as dependent on it as the industry to which it belonged.

Soon, however, and quite extraordinarily quickly, it grew up with industry. The first children of the first workers, as Landes remarks, already need twenty-two million pounds of yarn a generation later in 1787, more than eight times as much. Yet one must not think that the working class grew so very quickly, for the amount of work done went up simultaneously, since the individual worker could finish more cotton.

There is a curious point to consider here. When England's cotton industry was still small and insignificant in 1760, the woollen industry already had a great past behind it. For centuries it had been the most important industry in England. The earliest machines to be invented were 'quite naturally' intended for the woollen industry, and both Kay's flying shuttle and Hargreaves' Jenny were often used in this industry.[8] But after that there was scarcely any progress in the development of the woollen industry,[9] so that the system of domestic production was maintained, and we must stand by our statement that the cotton industry was the first factory industry. We also stand by our statement that the early proletariat was from the cotton industry.

This cotton industry proletariat in England was born in a social landscape which had possessed a capitalist character for a long time; a feature which distinguished England from the whole of the European continent.

We are now in a position to distinguish between conditions of general capitalism and of specifically industrial capitalism. The England of pre-industrial capitalism, or pre-1760 England, naturally had free wage labourers in large numbers as well as capitalists who considered it to be their function to accumulate capital, and who did not spend their income on senseless luxuries like the feudal rulers of France. England's free wage labourers were men who had already become accustomed if not to the rhythm of machine-working, nevertheless to the combination of

THE RIVALS.

A *Punch* cartoon, 1846.　　Prize Peasant,　　*versus*　　Prize Pig.

personal freedom, mobility and an economic obligation to work. This process had been completed in the sixteenth and seventeenth centuries. Hence the ruling classes of England in about 1760 had a great deal of experience in controlling the supply and discipline of free workers. They had worked out an entire system, a gigantic code of working rules specially devised for free workers.

The new bourgeoisie of the machine industry was able to rely on all this when its task was to accustom workers trained for work under general capitalist conditions to the discipline of the machine and the factory.

It was of course an upheaval in the lives of the workers when the centre of industrial production was transferred to the towns with steam replacing water as the source of power. It was of course an upheaval in their lives when the growth of the towns forced them to give up even their 'rural gardens' which they had owned, even in the towns, until 1810, and in many cases 1820; but naturally the suppression of such a confined group of unhappy and unfortunate people constantly set new and difficult problems for the ruling classes.

However, before machines were introduced in England, at least he transition had been completed: the transition from feudally ied labour to free capitalist labour, from work measured primarily by the amount done to work based on a time-unit, from work which chained a man in one specific locality and according to his accomplishments to work forced on him primarily by economic pressure – in other words, without work he could not live.

The working classes in the England of 1760, like their fore-athers before them, had already had an introduction to capitalist dependence and work discipline. This is the fundamental difference between the modern workers in England and those of all other countries; the same difference exists between the capitalists of England, with all their experience based on capitalist development without machines, and the capitalists of all other nations.

Workers and capitalists, then, entered the age of the Industrial Revolution much earlier than in any other country. This difference was obviously most marked during the first generation of the Industrial Revolution, whenever this was in the four countries here reviewed. If we place the beginning of the Industrial Revolution in England in 1760, and hence the beginning of the second generation of modern industrial workers in about 1785, this corresponds with the period, let us say, from 1790 to 1815 in France. From 1790 to 1815 the workers in France had in general to learn the capitalist labour discipline of free men and women, and in particular that of the 'appendage to the machine', a special kind of free citizen.

At the same time the comparison of generations in England and France throws into relief another special feature of the English revolution. At a time when a working class was being formed in France and Germany, there was in England a working class of the second and third generation. But this is not merely a difference in generations. It is a basic difference, in as much as England already had an 'hereditary proletariat' when the working classes were in the process of formation on the Continent: these were modern workers who were the children of modern workers, industrial workers who had grown up in industry, whether as child-employees or merely as part of the whole atmosphere.

In about 1785 this hereditary proletariat was, of course, still quite small. Even a generation later, about 1810, it was certainly still a minority, as there was such a large influx into industry from every interested class and walk of life. It was still possible too to escape modern industry, for parents might hand the child over to a craft-apprenticeship or send him to relations in the country. In addition, the change to another class or grade, even to become a small capitalist, was certainly not yet a strange occurrence.

Thus, however important it may be to state that England had at its disposal an 'hereditary proletariat' much earlier than other countries, one should not rush into a premature search for this new wonder of modern society. Though it might be logical to wish to search for it at the end of the eighties, one should not count on finding it very widespread before 1820 – partly because factories were inundated with new arrivals in the work-force, partly because there was still considerable movement between classes and grades.

So long as workers (in the old sense) lived under feudal obligations, they were only separated from one another, albeit widely separated, by the nature of those obligations. The journeyman who was feudally tied, and shackled to a guild, was subject to quite different rules of life from the one who was tied to the land and again from the inmate of a spinning-house and penitentiary. These peculiarly feudal barriers erected between grades and classes, which were found in France, Germany, Holland, Italy, Spain and Austria, did not exist in capitalist, pre-industrial England. Freedom of movement succeeded in bringing the different grades from which the modern working classes were later recruited, closer than they ever could on the Continent. In spite of all the barriers separating them, to transfer from one grade to another was easier, for they were not so exclusive as in feudal countries. Certain feelings of fellowship, sympathy and solidarity developed among them.

The Irish. On the other hand, the modern working class was from the very beginning more deeply divided than those of Germany and France, and for the very simple reason that England was the only country in Europe which had a European colony, whose people were also comfortably settled in England itself: namely, Ireland.

Ireland had been living for several centuries in the most terrible poverty, plundered by English estate-owners, and to all intents and purposes subjugated. While Pope surveyed the world with great satisfaction and found it to be both reasonable and good (seen from London), his good friend Swift (from Dublin) was cursing the colonial overlord England in lines of the bitterest irony. In the history of anti-colonial literature one work by Swift stands alone. In this he wonders how his homeland is to be saved, and here is a brief *résumé* of it.

He starts with the bold statement that out of one and a half million inhabitants of Ireland, there were some two hundred thousand fertile married couples, of whom about thirty thousand would be in a position to bring up their children, while fifty thousand had miscarriages or produced children who died from disease or accident. This left one hundred and twenty thousand married couples who produced superfluous children. But they were only superfluous if one was unskilful and did not know what to do with them. And here, Swift, political economist and eradicator of human misfortune, came forward with his suggestions which, in their angry irony, their bitterness down to the last detail, are without parallel in literature.

Of the hundred and twenty thousand superfluous children – for why should one not have a child per year if it is worth while? – one hundred thousand should be sold as meat for slaughter. Swift was thinking specially of the housewife and her table, for one had to be practical. A child, he thought, would be quite sufficient for an evening party to which one invited one's friends, while a child's hind-quarter would be perfectly sufficient for the smallest family circle. He was concerned for the housewife right from the time of purchase. His advice was that one should buy children like so

many fishes, preferably live, aged about one year and weighing around twenty eight pounds. Child-meat kept fresh for a fair length of time, according to the experiences of 'an American acquaintance of the author's'. If one portion were roasted on the day of purchase, the rest could be stewed and eaten on the fourth day, with pepper and salt to taste. Child was very suitable for the human palate and delicious when grilled or in a *fricassée* or *ragoût*. Besides, excellent gloves could be made out of child's skin. Also, mothers could make an annual profit of eight shillings on the birth of each baby, and so, instead of feeling the child to be a burden, could consider it a useful investment.

The following were to be rejected as quackish remedies – the crowning irony, for Swift now suggested methods of removing

Left For centuries in Ireland, colonial exploitation by England and the resulting poverty had kept a 'natural' kerb on the population, but even so the majority of Irish families were too big to support. *Below* Uneducated and unemployed – the indifference of the habitually oppressed.

Ireland's poverty which seemed to him both just and necessary: limiting consumption to articles of Irish manufacture; cutting imports of English luxury goods; the re-establishment of conditions of land-tenure which would not ruin tillers of the soil; ending political strife among the Irish in favour of a patriotic united front; a demand for Irish manufacture and its efficiency; for thrift, for taxation of foreign English estate-owners who spent their income outside the country; and so forth.

'A modest proposal' was what Swift called the essay[10] of 1729 in which he gave advice on how to solve Ireland's difficulties.

At the time of the Industrial Revolution, however, Ireland was exporting to England not slaughtered children, but workers. Engels wrote:

With a diet of potatoes, an aimless existence, and
temporary outlets in alcohol or violence, the young
Irishman had nothing to lose by emigrating to
England where he would find comparative riches.
For the industrialist, he would provide the cheapest
adult, unskilled labour available.

The swift expansion of English industry could not have taken place, if it
had not had a reserve to call on from the numerous and poor population
of Ireland. Irishmen had nothing to lose at home, and much to gain in
England, and ever since it had been known in Ireland that secure work
and good wages for the poor but able-bodied were to be found on the
eastern shore of the St George's Channel, crowds of Irishmen had been
coming across each year. It has been calculated that so far over one million
have immigrated in this way, and that another fifty thousand come over
annually. Almost all of these descend on the industrial areas, on the big
cities in particular, and there form the lowest stratum of the population.
Thus the number of poor Irishmen in London is one hundred and twenty
thousand, in Manchester forty thousand, in Edinburgh twenty-nine thousand.[11] These people, who have grown up with practically no civilisation,
accustomed to privations of all kinds from their youth up, uncouth, ad-
dicted to drink, careless of the future, come over in this state and bring all
their coarse habits with them into a class of the English population which
is not particularly attracted to a good upbringing or moral principles.[12]

And then he quotes Carlyle:

The wild Milesian[13] features, looking false ingenuity, restlessness, unreason,
misery and mockery, salute you on all highways and byways. The English
coachman, as he whirls past, lashes the Milesian with his whip, curses him
with his tongue. The Milesian is holding out his hat to beg. He is the sorest
evil this country has to strive with. In his rags and laughing savagery, he
is there to undertake all work that can be done by mere strength of hand
and back: for wages that will purchase him potatoes. He needs only salt
for condiment: he lodges to his mind in any pig-hutch or dog-hutch, roosts
in outhouses: and wears a suit of tatters, the getting off and on of which is
said to be a difficult operation transacted only in festivals and the high-
tides of the calendar. The Saxon man if he cannot work on these terms,
finds no work. The uncivilised Irishman, not by his strength but by the
opposite of strength drives out the Saxon native, takes possession in his
room. There abides he, in his squalor and unreason, in his falsity and
drunken violence, as the ready-made nucleus of degradation and disorder.
Whosoever struggles, swimming with difficulty, may now find an example
how the human being can exist not swimming but sunk.

That the condition of the lower multitude of English labourers approxi-
mates more and more to that of the Irish competing with them in all markets; that whatsoever labour, to which mere strength with little skill will

suffice, is to be done, will be done not at the English price, but at an approximation to the Irish price: at a price superior as yet to the Irish, that is, superior to scarcity of third-rate potatoes for thirty weeks yearly, superior, yet hourly, with the arrival of every new steamboat, sinking nearer to an equality with that – who is blind to all this?[14]

Engels adds:

If we overlook the exaggerated, one-sided condemnation of the Irish national character, Carlyle is quite right. These Irish workers who come over to England for fourpence – on the decks of the steamers where they often stand packed like cattle – are settling everywhere. The very worst lodgings are quite good enough for them; their clothes give them little cause for concern as long as they hold together by a thread. Shoes are unknown to them; their food is potatoes, only potatoes. Any balance of their earnings they drink away; what use has such a race for wages? The worst districts of all the big cities are inhabited by Irishmen; anywhere that a region is conspicuous by being particularly filthy or dilapidated, one can be quite sure of seeing mainly these Celtic faces, which are quite different from the Anglo-Saxon features of the natives; and of hearing the sing-song, aspirated Irish brogue, which the true Irishman never loses.[15]

This shows first that English factory-owners with Irishmen were dealing with workers who were much cheaper than English workers, but who, in spite of their being unbelievably poorly paid by English standards, nevertheless felt justifiably that they could live better in England than in Ireland.

It also shows that English workers had competitors among the Irish who had a constant effect on the standard of living and acted as wage-reducers, while the English workers (what Engels calls 'the exaggerated and one-sided condemnation of the Irish national character' was in one form or another common to the overwhelming majority of the English nation) looked down on the Irish as an 'inferior race' and 'felt better' in doing so; they frequently felt closer to their own capitalists than to the Irish worker. What we call class solidarity was broken. The Irish were the 'English niggers' and just as white unemployed and capitalists together lynched the 'niggers' in Georgia, so in England at the time of the Industrial Revolution there was not infrequently an 'ideological union' between 'labour and capital' against the Irish.

But while this peculiarity of the English development, compared with the continent of Europe, quite understandably caused a particularly rapid reduction of wage-rates in England, one important point must not be forgotten. The long period of pre-industrial development of capitalism had brought England quite an appreciable improvement in the standard of living, while on the Continent the period before the Industrial Revolution was filled with years of decline in feudal society, and this in its turn imposed its burden on all operatives. When, in a book on the history of food conditions in England, one reads: 'for the first fifty years of the [eighteenth] century fortune smiled on most of the people of England',[16] one feels that the language is decidedly too cheerful; but the sentence contains substantially more than a grain of truth. Moreover, by about seventeen hundred, the wages of workers in England were higher than on the Continent, which was certainly not the case in the sixteenth and the beginning of the seventeenth century. This is partly to be accounted for by the gradual and general worsening of the condition of operatives on the Continent in the years from 1650 to 1760, but partly too by a definite improvement of their condition in England. An interesting and indirect piece of evidence for the relatively better situation of workers in England compared with the continent, is furnished by the author of an article on the 'miseries of the poor',[17] which states that the wages in France and Holland were lower than in England, and that one could only improve the conditions of the poor in England if they earned lower wages, thereby increasing England's ability to compete with the Continent.

Pre-industrial capitalism. Another special feature of the evolution of a working class stems from the long pre-industrial development of capitalism in England. This pre-industrial development had been used by the English land-owning class primarily to procure ideal capitalist conditions for production on 'their' land through the active eradication of the small-producers, the peasant-proprietors. Trevelyan is inclined to play down the destruction of the yeoman[18] and to describe it as having taken longer than it really did; and he observes:

The early Georgian village represented, on the whole, a healthy economic and social order, but with the defect that the power of the great landowners was on the increase instead of yielding to a more diffused system of land-ownership and a larger measure of village autonomy. Even in the reigns of the first two Georges, the small yeomen freeholders and the small squires were declining in numbers. The great period of the yeomen freeholders and of small, compact estates was the Tudor and Stuart epoch. In Anne's reign the acquisitive tendency of the large landowners was becoming more than ever marked. The squires were jealous of the small freeholders as being politically and socially independent of their sway. The rage for game-preserving, characteristic of the epoch, made them look askance at a fellow without a coat-of-arms who had the impudence to shoot partridge on his own patch of ground. Indeed the squirearchical Parliaments of the later Stuarts had most tyrannically passed game laws which excluded all freeholders of under a hundred pounds a year from killing game even on their own land.

To buy out the small freeholder was an even more satisfactory way of disposing of him. For his part, he often thought he might do better in the modern world than by staying on his farm. All through the eighteenth century yeomen families were drifting to the towns.[19]

Poets like Oliver Goldsmith who wrote his *The Deserted Village* at the beginning of the Industrial Revolution (1770), or George Crabbe with *The Village* (1783) went much further in their accounts of the depopulation of the countryside. Cobbett wrote in 1825 about the enclosures of the past, which have

almost extinguished the race of small farms; from one end of England to the other, the houses which formerly contained little farms and their happy families are now seen sinking into ruins, all the windows except one or two stopped up [because of the window tax], leaving just enough for some labourer, whose father was, perhaps, the small farmer, to look back upon his half-naked and half-famished children, while, from his door, he surveys all around him the land teeming with the means of luxury to his opulent and overgrown master.[20]

This is what, with a wry and bitter smile, the countryfolk said:

> The law locks up the man or woman
> Who steals the goose from off the common;
> But leaves the greater villain loose
> Who steals the common from the goose.

In such circumstances the drift from the land into industry should have played a less significant rôle than elsewhere. And yet I am not sure whether that was really the case, for to some extent the last great wave of expropriation belonged to the Industrial Revolution – or at any rate stopped before it ended for want of numbers. Brentano remarked that 'the British peasant class had been destroyed by the beginning of the nineteenth century.'[21] Hence one can at least claim that the main characteristic of the last period

Above The poacher's family plead for his life. Strict game laws typified the situation: those who once had had a small farm were now at the mercy of those who bought them out.
Right Officially the agricultural worker was ignored.

of the Industrial Revolution in England was the relatively small influx of peasants into the nascent working class.

Now if one combined the two peculiarities which have been here revealed – the violent influx of uprooted colonial workers accustomed to a very low standard of living, and the relatively small influx of peasants accustomed for hundreds of years to a steady way of life, regulated only by nature's laws – the result is a particularly unstable working class. This naturally runs counter to the other fact, that, over a period of centuries, a very large number of workers had been accustomed to an industrialist and capitalistic labour-discipline.

If in addition we count miners as members of the working class in a wider sense and remember their way of life (barbaric and isolated), and if we further consider the fact that during the whole of the Industrial Revolution mining played a particularly large part in England, we then have the picture of a working class whose character had been slightly modified, and which in many respects was moving in the direction it had been forced to follow through the enormous influx of Irish workers.

In order to fill in the picture from another point of view, we should consider the ironworkers, who, in a wider sense like the miners, could already be included in the working class, though they did not use mechanical tools to any great extent. The iron industry played an important part in England's non-agricultural production. Cole observes:

For a long time miners and ironworkers continued to be thought of by most people as simply labourers and were in fact drawn largely from the ranks of agricultural workers, whereas the factories were observed to be replacing old domestic trades and agglomerating their workers into towns . . . Miners and heavy metal-workers were often looked on as a race of savages, set apart from the rest of society.[22]

This does not, of course, refer to the metalworkers in the big cities. In 1770 Bowden drew attention to a letter of Matthew Boulton, James Watts' partner, which reads: 'I have trained up

Above St Hilda's colliery, near Durham.
Below Trolley-boys at work in the mines. If those
in the towns thought of miners
as 'a race of savages', they, in their tightly-knit
communities often influenced by religious
sects, saw the mill-towns as dens of evil.

many and am training up more plain country lads into good workmen.'[23] Besides, I think it not improbable that mining villages were to be found, in Scotland, Wales and elsewhere, where there was so much respectability (thanks frequently to the influence of religious sects) that many a rural market town with, perhaps, one mill seemed to be a sink of iniquity compared with the mining village.

It follows that, however justified one may be in using Irish influence and the prominent part played by miners and iron-workers to highlight special anarchical features of the English working class way of life, one may only do so if one indicates the subtle differences existing within these strata and groups brought about by religious 'heresy' – for the Catholic Irish were obviously just as heretical or sectarian as numerous Protestant groups not conforming to the Church of England or the Church of Scotland. It was the sectarian influence which was mainly responsible for large sections of the workers, unsatisfied by the official church, either turning to these sects or becoming atheists, or at any rate 'non-church'. A religious census in 1851 produced the information that only twenty-five per cent of the population went to church. And Le Play in the same year confirmed with astonishment 'an almost complete absence of religious feeling', when he investigated the life of English working families, and wrote about it in a work entitled *On the Insufficient Religious Education given to English Workers*.[24] Yet even a clergyman and social reformer, Kingsley had declared in his *Politics for the People*:

'We have been using the Bible as a police handbook – like a dose of opium to keep beasts of burden quiet while being loaded – as a book to keep discipline among the poor.'

Thanks also to the Protestant sects (not of course to the Roman Catholic Church) a larger proportion of the labouring sections of the population who formed the new working class were able to read than on the Continent. For independent reading of the Bible was often one of the features which distinguished sects from the Established Church. This feature disappeared in the Industrial

Revolution, when pious artisans, workers in domestic industry and outworkers were absorbed in the 'great concourse of the factory proletariat'. Hence it is highly probable that the Industrial Revolution in England, as opposed to the continent of Europe, in which it could no longer take root, caused an increase in illiteracy.

Density of city population. In conclusion, one should consider the figures in Table 6.[25] It will be seen that the density of population in cities in England was far greater than anywhere else in the world. In Germany there was no city among the first five (except the

Table 6. Population of the five largest cities with the exception of the capital, in 1850.

Britain		France	
Manchester	400,000	Marseille	195,000
Liverpool	375,000	Lyon	175,000
Glasgow	330,000	Bordeaux	130,000
Birmingham	235,000	Rouen	100,000
Leeds	175,000	Nantes	95,000
Germany		**United States**	
Hamburg	170,000	Philadelphia	22,000†
Breslau	115,000	Baltimore	170,000
Munich	100,000	Boston	135,000
Dresden	95,000	St Louis	80,000
Cologne	95,000	Pittsburg	70,000

* Not including New York, which, in U.S.A., has the status of a European capital.
† 1840.

capital, Berlin) which equalled the fifth largest in England; in the U.S.A. (except for New York) and likewise in France (with the exception of Paris) no city approached the fourth largest in England.

But if we compare the capitals (in the U.S.A., New York) the following are the 1850 figures:

London	2,400,000
Paris	1,100,000
New York	700,000
Berlin	400,000

It follows that all the ills which were brought about by the enormous growth of cities during the Industrial Revolution and later were mainly concentrated in England; besides, the difference between England and the other cities in the first half of the century had widened quite considerably. Finally, it must not be forgotten that in 1800, apart from some of the capitals, the following cities, in order of size, had 100,000 or more inhabitants in the four countries under consideration:

Marseille	110,000
Lyon	110,000
Hamburg	100,000

Among these there is not one English or American city. One can see what went on in England between 1800 and 1850. One can see what a social change this very intensive urbanising process must have had. Living conditions were worse than anywhere else in the world, and so were what might be called the moral conditions, in the broadest meaning of this word.

Thus if the standard of living of the operatives in England in 1760 was undoubtedly much higher than on the Continent, the condition of the workers in 1850 was far worse than on the Continent; whereas the petty bourgeoisie and the bourgeois middle class enjoyed a standard of living far above the Continental level.

The United States: a special case

The United States is a special case for it could be doubted whether it ought to be discussed in this book. The doubt arises because one has to consider carefully whether by 1850 a working class had emerged in the U.S.A.

This is the argument: in Europe, workers were faced with the alternatives of finding employment as workers or begging, that is, starving. Since begging by the able-bodied could be punished, and starving did not seem to be a practical alternative, there was only one choice left, to yield to economic pressure and find employment as workers. In the United States, on the other hand, there was still the possibility of escaping the worker's life by settling on the land and becoming a farmer. So even if one could get temporary employment as a worker, being a labourer was not a permanent job and had no fixed status or function in society.

We find an example of this reasoning in the appendix to the American edition of the *Condition of the labouring class in England* of 1886[26]:

There were two factors which for a long time prevented the inevitable consequences of the capitalist system in America from being revealed in their true light. These were the access to ownership of cheap land and the flood of immigrants. They enabled the great mass of indigenous Americans, for years on end, to 'retire' from wage-labour at an early age and to become farmers, dealers or even entrepreneurs, whereas the hard lot of the wage-labourer with his status of proletarian for life, fell mostly on the immigrant. But America has grown out of this early phase, the limitless virgin forests have disappeared and the still more limitless prairies are passing more and more rapidly out of the hands of the nation and the states into those of private owners. The great safety-valve against the rise of a permanent proletarian class has effectively ceased to operate.

Even a whole succession of immigrants succeeded in withdrawing themselves from the ranks of the workers. 'The north and east complained about the departure of young people and new immigrants' was how a history of rural politics in the U.S.A. put it.[27]

Slums in Ragpickers' Court, New York. In theory, the open spaces of the western U.S.A. could have absorbed the over-crowding of the eastern cities, but the lack of means and agricultural equipment often made the journey westwards a practical impossibility.

On the other hand one must not forget that freedom to settle was often only theoretically possible; for how was a worker from the east 'simply' to cross the continent in order to settle under difficult natural conditions, with the expectation of considerable capital investment in far-off regions which were favoured by the complete absence of a land monopoly? And the further the 'west' became separated from the east, the harder the move. Some time after the last of the years we are reviewing, the *Workingman's Advocate* of 2 July 1870, when dealing with the question sometimes asked, why the unemployed did not 'go west', observed:

Firstly, not many have the means to go there, and secondly, they have nothing with which to work the land when they arrive . . . If they could till the land without oxen or horses or agricultural implements, or could live on grass, shrubs and wild fruit while the first harvest was ripening, the 'way to the west' would be a problem one could think about seriously.

Samuel Young certainly exaggerated when he argued that the mass of the population in Europe was condemned to hunger and poverty, while in the United States the population could continue to increase and live comfortably, thanks to the great public ownership of land.[28] That is a one-sided view. But the important point about this problem is that it really has two sides. Marx writes at the end of the first volume of *Capital*:

On the one hand the vast and continuous stream of humanity driven to America, year in, year out, leaves its coagulated sediments behind it in the east of the United States, while the wave of emigration from Europe casts men more quickly on to the labour market there than the wave of emigration westwards can wash them away . . .

This means that while of course a large number of men emigrated westwards, the mobility of operatives and the opportunities for their absorption in the west were not sufficient to relieve the situation in the eastern labour market, and to offset the depressing influence of immigration on the industrial workers' standard of living. What Mitchell[29] observed in 1860 was already beginning to take effect in the thirties:

While the West has been calling for labourers, workmen and agriculturists of all grades, there have been large numbers of superfluous young men hanging about in the large eastern cities, competing for poorly paid employment.

It was by no means so easy to escape the poverty in the eastern towns by migrating westwards. This was also pointed out by land-propagandists of the 1840s – George Henry Evans, for example – who demanded completely free distribution of land expressly for the purpose of improving the position of the workers in the east.[30] The starting point of their argument was that the actual extent of absorption of workers as peasants or farmers in the western regions of the continent, which were growing in size and scope, was not bringing sufficient or effective relief to the workers' situation in eastern industry. Besides, investigations by Goodrich and Davison[31] show that the migrants to the west came to a great extent from the country and not from the towns.

How then is the main question to be answered? Can one say that a working class had been formed in the United States by 1850? Or may one merely state that the process of development had made striking progress by then?

To my mind the second question, at least, can be answered in the affirmative, and perhaps the first one as well, from a purely local point of view, and perhaps as far as the textile plants of New England were concerned. Despite all the mobility between the various groups and grades, despite a general mobility in Europe between the ruling and oppressed classes, though only during the years of revolution, one could in 1850 speak of workers in clear, definite terms; and every worker in Manchester would recognise and approve a worker from Lowell as a class comrade. Only one must not forget that in the Industrial Revolution Manchester was characteristic of England, but Lowell, if it represented New England, was certainly not characteristic of the States.

In any case one must bear in mind that the special feature of the working class between 1760 and 1850 was that their status as workers was not hereditary. Committed and homogeneous working families were in a small minority. An hereditary proletariat,

Table 7. Immigrants to U.S.A.

Year	English per cent	Irish per cent	German per cent	Workers per cent	Businessmen per cent	Engineers and farmers per cent
1820	1,782	3,974	948	9	25	31
1825	1,002	5,857	448	10	29	32
1830	733	3,105	1,972	12	25	41
1835	468	29,350	8,245	15	20	55
1840	318	41,704	28,581	22	12	63

such as one found on the continent of Europe and in England, did not generally exist.

When we were dealing with the question just discussed, the problem of the enormous numbers of immigrants was also mentioned. The influx took on such proportions that, according to the census of 1850, 2,240,000 Americans – about ten per cent of the population – were born abroad. It should not be a matter for surprise that a quarter of the population were either born abroad or were at least children of mixed or purely foreign parents.

The annual immigration totals were:

Three-year period	Numbers
1819–22*	8,100
1838–40	63,700
1841–43	79,100
1844–46	115,800
1847–49	252,800

*October to September.

A considerable number of these immigrants, as has been mentioned above, did not at first penetrate very far inland, but remained in the eastern towns; while those who went further westwards often found a similar type of employment to those who stayed in the east, in the factory industry. Although the agricultural regions of the United States also provided a large number of industrial workers, it would not be surprising to find, at least in the forties, that more additional workers came from overseas than from the American countryside.

Bromwell's analysis of the main nationalities and trades of the immigrants can be seen above in Table 7.[32]

German immigrants to Salt Lake City, at Castle Garden, New York. Most immigrants did not at first go far inland, and those who did often found themselves similarly employed in factory industries.

As far as the country of origin of the immigrants was concerned, the numbers fluctuated from year to year. On the whole though, the numbers of Englishmen decreased, and those of the Germans and Irishmen increased sharply. The percentages by trades are to be viewed with great caution. Engineers were probably skilled workers from numerous trades; farmers were peasants such as land-labourers and other unskilled workers, who wanted to go into agriculture from the very start. Doubtless the numbers of 'businessmen', including the large numbers of unemployed, entrepreneurs, etc., decreased during the period, while the percentage of workers, skilled or unskilled, rose. Whether the percentage of farmers rose is hard to say.

To a certain extent immigration was forced on the country by American capitalists, not least with the object of lowering wages in the United States. Seth Luther, the well-known champion of legislation for the protection of workers, maintained that the entrepreneurs were sending 'agents to Europe, to induce foreigners to come here to underwork American citizens'.[33]

It is undeniable that the standard of living and conditions of work of many of these immigrants were bad. Even so enthusiastic a reporter on the workers' life in the United States as Murray describes the conditions prevalent among the immigrants as follows:

Among the thousands and tens of thousands whom the tide of emigration annually pours into the Atlantic seaports, and many of whom arrive without money or friends, or health, or skill wherewith to procure subsistence, great numbers suffer the extremities of hardship and want, especially in the neighbourhood of the towns where they are set ashore.[34]

It was reported in a series of articles in the *London Morning Chronicle*, (on 5 and 19 January and 12 February 1852) that many immigrants were afraid of being 'condemned to everlasting poverty'.[35]

The Irish formed a special group in the immigrants' ranks. The Irish immigrants remained for the most part permanently in the east, and many of them, unskilled and often illiterate, were

employed on the construction of canals and roads, and later in building stretches of railway. Thus for example, in 1818, three thousand Irishmen were put to work on the construction of the Erie canal. Matthew Carey, father of the famous economist Henry C. Carey, made a detailed account of the wages, and a more general one of the conditions, of the Irish workers, when he wrote in a broadsheet of 1829:

Thousands of our laboring people travel hundreds of miles in quest of employment on canals at $62\frac{1}{2}$ cents to $87\frac{1}{2}$ cents per day, paying $1.50 to $2.00 a week for board, leaving families behind depending upon them for support. They labor frequently in marshy grounds, where they inhale pestiferous miasmata, which destroy their health, often irrevocably. They return to their poor families broken-hearted, and with ruined constitutions, with a sorry pittance, most laboriously earned, and take to their beds, sick and unable to work. Hundreds are swept off annually, many of them leaving numerous and helpless families. Notwithstanding their wretched fate, their places are quickly supplied by others, although death stares them in the face. Hundreds are most laboriously employed on turn-pikes, working from morning to night at from half a dollar to three-quarters a day, exposed to the broiling sun in summer and all the inclemency of our severe winters. There is always a redundancy of wood-pilers in our cities, whose wages are so low that their utmost efforts do not enable them to

The emigration office, Cork. As in England, the Irish immigrants to the United States found themselves at the bottom of the social ladder. Immigrants, especially Irish immigrants, were proletarians for life.

earn more than from thirty-five to fifty cents per day. ... Finally there is no employment whatever, how disagreeable or loathsome, or deleterious soever it may be, or however reduced the wages, that does not find persons willing to follow it rather than beg or steal.[36]

Some of the Irish immigrants were even lower on the social ladder than the Negroes. The *New York Herald* put out the following advertisement: 'Cook, laundryman and ironer required; must know his job perfectly; colour and country of origin immaterial; but no Irishmen'.[37] No wonder the Irish, in the New York elections, put out slogans like: 'Down with the Nagurs. Let them go back to Africa where they belong.'[38]

Negro slaves. In addition (and it follows from this last remark) there was the general problem of the Negroes, especially in so far as they were concerned as slaves.

The first Negroes to come to the U.S.A. were not slaves but 'indentured', that is, a sort of debtor-slave who was released after he had worked off the 'costs' of his passage. John Rolfe, the first tobacco-farmer in the U.S.A., wrote in 1619: 'About last August a Dutch man-o'-war came and sold us twenty Negroes'; who, as they were baptised, could not be slaves according to a current law (annulled in Virginia in 1667), but only 'Christian servants'. In 1650, thirty-one years after the arrival of the first shipload of Negroes in Jamestown, there were only three hundred Negroes in Virginia. The majority of these were 'indentured'; not until this period did slavery begin to be established and it was barely legalised before 1660.[39] A generation later, however, in 1680, the three hundred Negroes had already become three thousand, and at this time conditions regulating slave-ownership were established everywhere in the colonies, even though they numbered only two hundred in the whole of New England. But between 1680 and 1688, the English Royal African Company brought over ten thousand Negroes to America, about a quarter of whom died on the journey. Even in the seventeenth century, race-discrimination against Negroes was general; thus in 1664, a law was passed

in Maryland which enslaved white women who married Negroes, for as long as their husbands lived; but the children of such marriages were slaves 'for ever', and in 1686, the skilled workers and artisans of New York defended themselves successfully against the employment of Negroes and Indians (as slaves) in various occupations.[40]

Here we are dealing with true slavery, indistinguishable in character from the slavery of ancient times. The slave belonged to his master and the latter could do with him what he thought fit. It was true slavery in its consequences also, as it could not fail to lead to matriarchal tendencies within the Negro families: one was inclined to separate the father from the family, rather than the mother, to sell him or send him to other places of work. And yet this slavery was fundamentally different from that of the Ancients in that it helped the development of capitalism, and was used more and more by capitalists, who were capitalists in the sense that slave-owners were agents for a growing capitalist world market.

Sale of pictures and
slaves in the Rotunda,
New Orleans, 1842.

171

If however it is thought that slavery in the nineteenth century was limited for all practical purposes to the south, we must state categorically that in the first instance all that has been said about mobility between classes, mobility between trades and geographical mobility was also valid for the north and north-west. And on the subject of the ruling classes, it ought to be made clear that, while in the north there was a small number of capitalists dependent on a broad, not entirely uninfluential middle class, from which they were recruited, and into which individuals often fell back, there was in the south a narrow, closed and ancient aristocracy of slave-owners who held absolute sway. The total number of slave-owners on the eve of the Civil War was four hundred thousand, including members of the same family: about a quarter of the southern population. But fewer than seven per cent of the whites owned seventy-five per cent of all slaves, and the real power lay in the hands of about 1,700 slave-owners, each of whom possessed at least one hundred slaves. The great majority of the whites, however, lived in relatively poor circumstances economically, though they felt ideologically far superior to the Negroes. An American sociologist rightly remarks:

At least ninety per cent of four million negroes were kept illiterate as a necessary police measure. About a million poor whites, living largely in the rural slums created by the wasteful plantation system, were not much better off.[41]

Socially, however, the great slave-owners, rather like the Junkers in Prussia, played a special rôle which far outweighed their influence on the economy. This was very clearly illustrated by the fact that for fifty of the seventy-two years between Washington and Lincoln, the south provided the President, and twenty of the thirty-five Chief Justices of the country, and also that generally the majority of government officials came from there. The New York banker Clews correctly described the situations in Washington on the outbreak of the Civil War: 'About seven-eighths of the people of Washington at that time were southerners. The

office holders were largely composed of the latter and they were expecting to be suddenly turned out of office.'[42]

Indentured labour. In addition to the slaves at the beginning of the Industrial Revolution there were the indentured, a large section of the immigrants who had to hire themselves out in order to work off the costs of their passages and other expenses. Indentured employees were often kept for years in debtor-slavery, since the debts owed to the master were frequently subject to high interest-rates during the whole time of their repayment by labour. These work-revenues often provided the master with much more than slavery, for, with the indentured employees, he was in many cases dealing with skilled artisans from European countries. Their skill could be utilised by their masters at no cost during the years of their service, while

slaves had to hold out longer. Morris writes: 'Too often were indentured servants treated in a degrading manner and denied even a subsistence livelihood.'[43] Their numbers were relatively large. John R. Commons, Carter Goodrich, R. B. Morris and others think that about half the white immigrants had originally arrived indentured, and had worked off their debts, mostly the costs of their passage. Some of them were indebted to agents, captains, and so forth, who immediately sold them in the colonies at a profit of about fifteen per cent; sometimes they came from the colonies financed by future slave-drivers. Advertisements like the following, quoted by Bridenbaugh from the *News Letter* of 25 October 1733, were frequently to be found in the press:

One hundred men from the Palatinate will be delivered, each for five years, to anyone ready to pay the passage charges of ten pounds per head.[44]

The indentured servants formed the lowest grade of the whites.[45] Below them, naturally, were the slaves, mostly black.[46] This shows that in the States, in contrast with England and France, the manual workers of the Industrial Revolution were composed of those living in various stages of personal freedom and serfdom.

In 1770, probably about a fifth of the population were slaves. If we estimate the number of indentured servants to be about fifteen per cent, we arrive at a figure of about two-thirds of the population who were free.[47] If we exclude sixty-seven per cent of these, who cannot be counted as employees, we finish with about sixty per cent, or three-fifths of the population, who were free employees.

The percentage of freemen was naturally higher in the north and lower in the south. A census in Maryland in 1755 gave the figures listed in Table 8.

Morris, who quotes this table, remarks[48] that freed indentured servants might be found sometimes among those 'in service'. In any case it can be seen that in 1755 less than three-fifths of the employees in Maryland were free (except for those who were not counted as workers). As far as the condition of the indentured servants and slaves is concerned, Maryland's share of slaves, especially in the south of the state, was substantially larger than in the north of the country, where the percentage of indentured servants was greater.

In the course of time the situation changed in favour of the freemen. At the time of the adoption of the state law, arrangements for indentured servants were not yet abolished. They officially disappeared in the course of the first twenty years of the nineteenth century, but in practice debtor-slavery continued in one form or another during the whole period under discussion, though it was less widespread.

As far as slavery is concerned, what follows is of interest. To begin with, the proportion of Negroes to the whole population fell, as we can see from Table 9.[49] The number of whites rose by about five hundred and twenty per cent; the number of 'non-whites'

Table 8. Maryland census figures, 1755.

	Free	Servants	Convicts	Total
Men	24,058	3,576	1,507	29,141
Women	23,521	1,824	386	25,731
Boys	26,637	1,049	67	27,753
Girls	24,141	422	21	24,584
Total Whites	98,357	6,871	1,981	107,209
Negroes				46,356

Table 9. Population of U.S.A. according to colour.

Year	Whites	Non-whites
1790	3,170,000	760,000
1810	5,860,000	1,380,000
1830	10,540,000	2,330,000
1850	19,550,000	3,640,000

Table 10. Composition of Negro population in U.S.A.

Year	Total	Free	Slaves
1790	760,000	60,000	700,000
1810	1,380,000	190,000	1,190,000
1830	2,330,000	320,000	2,010,000
1850	3,640,000	430,000	3,200,000

176

(in practice, only Negroes) about three hundred and eighty per cent.

Among the Negroes the percentage of slaves diminished (see Table 10).[50] In 1790, about eight per cent of the Negroes were free, in 1850 about twelve per cent – a slow rise over sixty years – while the actual number of slaves increased four and a half times.

Was there a 'working class' in the United States? It is clear that a working class with this sort of composition is somewhat peculiar: its geographical cohesion is in fact impossible; it cannot help being split up locally, it is theoretically larger and more comprehensive than it is in practice, and objective features which come to light from the process of production tell us very little from the ideological point of view.

According to their position in the production-process, even by their trade, and also in the amount of free time they have, these three classes may not show any differences: the grandson, born in the U.S.A., of an English colonist; an Irish emigrant; and a Negro. But their social position, their way of life, their ideology (including for example, their religion and the school they attended) cause them to live worlds apart. The Anglo-Saxon may have a field-marshal's baton in his knapsack even if he was not born with a silver spoon in his mouth. The Irishman can at best become a mayor, but with a tenth of the chances of the Anglo-Saxon dollar-millionaire, if the latter conducts his business skilfully. But he can neither be President, nor (as a Catholic) can he belong to the 'fashionable' clubs. The Negro is in any event condemned to social vegetation. And as soon as one leaves the worst slums, Irishmen are not even to be seen living in the same house, even if they are workers.

And so, should one talk about a working class?

If we go to a cotton factory in New England, the Hamilton Manufacturing Company, and study the geographical origin of the labour-force, we find the figures listed in Table 11.[51] Before the terrible famine-years in Ireland, immigration to the States

Table 11. Hamilton Manufacturing Company (New England): origin of labour force.

Origin	1 July 1830– 31 Dec 1830 1176 persons per cent	20 Jan 1835– 4 Dec 1836 1213 persons per cent	2 Oct 1839– 23 Apr 1845 516 persons per cent	28 Mar 1849– 18 Oct 1850 669 persons per cent
Massachusetts	82·2	41·3	49·4	21·1
New England	14·1	54·6	45·6	44·8
Other regions of the U.S.A.	0·0	0·3	0·0	2·2
Total for U.S.A.	96·3	96·2	95·0	68·2
Ireland	2·6	2·6	3·1	24·4
England	1·1	0·0	0·2	4·8
Canada	0·0	1·2	1·8	2·7

layed scarcely any part in the industry of New England despite he considerable numbers involved. During the 1830s, however, nother factor began to play an important rôle: the recruiting-rea for the labour-force which had hitherto appeared to be nainly Massachusetts, the home of the factory, had spread o the whole of New England, especially New Hampshire, Vermont nd Maine. Later the percentage of Irish exceeded the percentage oming from Massachusetts, and the percentage of Canadians

equalled that of New England, with the exception of Massachusetts. Hence the fluctuation seems to have been very strong at least among skilled workers. Gibb reports that of thirty-one machine operators employed in the Boston Manufacturing Company in May 1817 only five were still there in September 1823.[5] This was, perhaps, the effect of their stronger position which enabled them to find work elsewhere without much difficulty. It is difficult to imagine how unskilled workers, still so home-bound in their work during this period, still compelled to go to the same church as their superiors and subjected in others ways to a tyranny of ideas and traditions, could have changed their jobs so easily.

We mentioned above the worker who came to Lowell from Manchester. He would naturally find much that was different in character from his home town and a great deal would seem strange to him. But there is no doubt that he would be meeting

View of Pawtucket, Rhode Island,
one of the first centres of the
American cotton industry.

179

with members 'of his own class', of the same mind and in the same position as himself, with whom he would have no difficulty in making himself understood. Here in New England there was a working class which cohered at least as well as the one in old England. It was probably even more closely knit and welded together, if one considers its function in the process of production, the social position of its members, and its ideological character. No one in New England would have any doubt at all that he was faced with a working class – which had all the misery we are familiar with in Europe at the time of the Industrial Revolution. The following evidence, probably unique in literature, of the wretched state of the workers should be quoted:

> Office of Norfolk County Health
> Insurance Company,
> Lower Floor,
> Merchants' Exchange,
> Boston.
> July 27 1849

Mr C. V. N. Brundige,

Sir,
We have determined not to take any more applications, especially from the factories. Such places have been the graves of other companies, and we mean to avoid them. From what few policies we have there, we are constantly receiving claims. Doubtless there may be some good subjects there, but, from past experience, it would seem there was not more than a grain of wheat to a bushel of chaff, we can't distinguish them.

> Yours,
> Steph. Baley.

So the factories were the graves of the Health Insurance companies, because sickness among factory workers was so widespread. But what was far worse was the fact that they represented the graves of the workers too. This is not mentioned in the letter, as it had no importance from the insurance companies' point of view so long as they refused to insure the workers.[53]

Another document is worth quoting, which will be the last in this connexion, since the chief aim here is not to show up the miserable way of life of American workers during the Industrial Revolution, where, broadly speaking, they showed no difference from the European workers, but to point out the peculiarities of development in the United States. Besides, the document dates from a somewhat later period (1865), which means that its contents hold equally true for the end of the period we are discussing. We quote it here principally because it is a document of true humanity, of an honest search for truth by men who speak with the voice of those who have helped to cause this misery, when events in history are viewed objectively. We are referring to the report by Senator Martin Griffin of Boston for the Judiciary Committee asked to consider the expediency of regulating and limiting the number of hours constituting a day's labour, 29 April 1865:

But there is another view of the subject, which is even more important to us as a people, than the mere increase of wealth, or the perfection of the mechanic arts – the protection, preservation and advancement of man. In this view, we feel that there is a solemn duty and responsibility resting upon us, and that we are called upon to atone for our apathy of the past by early and earnest action in the future. We have been surprised at the developments which the investigation has produced. No subject which has been before a committee of this legislature has elicited more important facts, or awakened a more lively or general interest – an interest of the most numerous class in the community, and one which has but too seldom, in our opinion, engaged the attention of our legislation – the condition of our producing classes. In common with the great majority of the community, we have approached this subject with an entire ignorance of it; and in the belief that there was not, nor could be, any need of investigation, much less of improvement or melioration in the condition of those whose labors have enriched us, and whose skill and genius in the arts have placed us in the vanguard of the nation. Investigation has dispelled this ignorance; and your Committee must bear testimony to the urgent necessity of action and reform in the matter. The evidence presented almost challenged belief. Certainly the Committee were astonished that, in the midst of progress and prosperity unparalleled; advancement in the arts and science; development in machinery for the saving of labor; progress in invention, and in the increase of wealth and material prosperity; yet Man, the producer of all these – 'the first great cause of all', was the least of all, and least understood. The result of this prosperity of which we boast – and which should be a blessing to us – has a tendency to make the conditions of the working man little else than a machine, with no thought of aspiration higher, in the language of one of the witnesses, 'than a slave; for,' he added, 'we are slaves; overworked, worn out and enfeebled by toil; with no time left us for improvement of mind or soul. Is it surprising that we are degraded and ignorant?'

This is really one of the worthiest documents ever to come out of a parliamentary committee. It gives a clear picture of the reaction of ignorant but humane men when they were finding out about the conditions of the workers.

It is precisely these bad conditions which justify the arguments of the slave-owners of the south, that the slaves are materially better off than the workers in the north. This would, in many cases, have been true, as one usually looks after property (slaves) better than 'things' (free workers), which belong to no one and which one can use so long as they are serviceable, and then throw them out on the street. Colwell asked: 'Which is the worse slave: the one who belongs to his master as a valuable possession and is carefully searched for when he runs away, or the one who can loaf around freely and in mutual competition runs the risk of being simply cast aside?'[54]

Even among those who stood up for improving the conditions of the industrial workers there were some muddle-headed ones, who, with only the material conditions in view, did not see any difference between the lot of the slaves and the free workers. Brisbane, a political dreamer and disciple of Fourier, was speaking in this vein when he said that so long as work continued to be an unpleasant thing, workers would have to be forced into it; therefore it made little difference whether one was a wage slave in the north or a negro slave in the south.[55] And Kellog even maintained that the conditions under which industrial workers were exploited were even worse than those of the slaves in the south.[56]

Two features of the American working class. In conclusion, there are perhaps two features which should be emphasised.

The first concerns their attitude towards the technical side. We have already pointed out that there were scarcely any cases of machine-breaking in the United States. In the period when machines were first introduced and tendencies towards Luddism arose, the shortage of workers was acute and the fear of 'competition from the machine' relatively slight. And since men were accustomed to intensive social mobility, even the transition of goods production from the home to the factory did not affect them so deeply as it did in Europe. Hence workers were not hostile towards the machines, and in some cases they even welcomed them. At the head of the first chapter of his book, *American and British Technology in the 19th Century*,[57] H. J. Habakkuk is perfectly justified in placing a quotation from Chevalier:

In Europe work is often wanting for the hands; here (that is, in the United States) hands are wanting for the work.[58]

Left Robert Fulton's *Clermont*, the world's first steam packet, sailed from New York to Albany in September 1807. *Below* Machinery Hall at the fifth annual exhibition of the United States Agricultural Society, 1857.

183

And the first sentence of this chapter in Habakkuk's book reads:

There is a substantial body of comment, by English visitors to America in the first half of the nineteenth century, which suggests that, in a number of industries, American equipment was, in some sense, superior to the English even at this period.

England was the workshop of the world, to be sure, but in the far smaller industry of the United States there were so many better-equipped concerns, not least because, in the attitude of all groups and classes of society, even the working class, towards the machine, there was a slight shade of difference compared with Europe.

The second feature to be considered separates the American working class from the European, but not from other groups and classes in the U.S.A., and is ideological by nature. A very large number of men came to America as rebels, politically or religiously discontent with the conditions in the old homeland: ideologically up in arms. Besides, the population of the colonies won their national independence in the first victorious anti-colonial war in modern times.

But as we are here dealing with a peculiar feature of the whole nation including all classes and groups, and in Europe this peculiarity was, if anything, characteristic only of small minorities, until the working class became the great rebels of society at the end of the Industrial Revolution. This led to a strange situation in the U.S.A.: what became a feature of the working classes in Europe was not in any way prominent within the U.S.A. during the period under discussion. Yet even in 1861 the bourgeoisie could wage a revolutionary war against the slave-owning society of the south!

It is quite certain that this situation, next to the un-hereditary character of the proletariat, was one of the chief reasons for the bourgeoisie's drawing up a whole army of brilliant radicals, from abolitionists to Locofocos, on the one hand; and on the other, for the fact that political workers' parties made scarcely any headway and that socialist groups stood side by side with all kinds of religious sects. Certainly ideologies were beginning to take shape, corresponding to the interests of the working class, but they were primarily economic in form and directed only sporadically, and without achieving much currency, against 'society' as it existed.

France: the revolutionary tradition

When Daladier in 1938 led France down the pathway to defeat by Hitlerite Germany and stood up in the Assembly in favour of a deal with Hitler, Flandin (later to be foreign minister of the Vichy government) declared himself on his side. In this speech Flandin, the embittered foe of the popular front, referred to himself as *fils de la Grande Révolution*.

The 1789 Revolution was so deep-rooted that even a hundred and fifty years later an outspoken enemy of all revolution like Flandin believed he could obtain a better hearing by calling himself the son of the Great Revolution.

One can imagine how much more directly the lustre of this truly great revolution must have influenced the rising working class, particularly if we consider that even at the end of this unique citizens' revolt there were signs of the emergence of an ideology, violently and bloodily opposed by the petty bourgeoisie round Robespierre, which contained the first germs of a working class ideology; we observe too that the end of the bourgeois revolution was possibly the beginning of the working class revolution, and that directly after Robespierre came Babeuf 'founder of one of the first militant communist parties, who, as fellow-traveller of Jacques Roux, Robespierre, Hébert, Danton, Chaumette, and Saint-Just, maintained his unique personality as he reached out impetuously across the fixed limits of the bourgeois revolution towards a distant future of the "Fourth Estate".'[59]

I think it is correct to say that the French working class differed from those of other countries during the Industrial Revolution by a particularly high degree of political maturity. That it was more politically-minded than the working class of any other country is unquestionable. One has only to compare the English and French utopian dreamers of socialism. Robert Owen was the complete pattern of an 'economic utopian'. He assembled his experiences as a brilliantly clever and completely successful capitalist, and he transferred them as far as he could with the cold crayon always near his warm heart, to his utopian societies and real communist communities. Engels, who held him in particularly high esteem, said of him:

Owenite communism emerged in this purely business way, the fruit, so to speak, of commercial calculation. It maintained the same practical character throughout. Thus Owen, in 1823, suggested that Irish poverty should be removed by communist communities, and included complete calculations of the cost of construction, annual outlay and foreseeable revenue. So in his final plan for the future, the technical elaboration of details, including ground-plan, elevation and perspective, was presented with such practical knowledge that, given the Owen method of social reform, there was not very much that could be said against the detailed preparations themselves from a professional point of view.[60]

Engels, on the other hand – and one might almost say naturally – introduced notes about Saint-Simon in these words:

Saint-Simon was a child of the great French Revolution; at its outbreak he
was not yet thirty years old. The Revolution was the victory of the Third
Estate, that is, the great mass of the people engaged in production and trade,
over the two hitherto privileged and idle estates, the nobility and the clergy.

Then, passing to the *Geneva Letters*, to show that they win his
admiration for this statement, he said:

Saint-Simon, in his *Geneva Letters*, was already advancing the principle that
"all men should work". In the same work he recognised that the reign of
terror was the rule by the propertyless masses. 'Just look', he shouted to
them, 'what happened in France at the time your friends were in control;
they caused a famine.' Nevertheless, to consider the French Revolution as a
class struggle, not merely between the nobility and the bourgeoisie, but also
between the nobility, the bourgeoisie and the have-nots, was in 1802 a
discovery of genius.

Two anonymous French cartoons, 1789.
Left The Third Estate awakening from his
long slumber and casting off his chains.
Below After the capture of the Bastille, the
Third Estate – with Justice on his side –
outweighs the clergy and the nobility.

The transition from Saint-Simon to Fourier was treated in this way:

If, in Saint-Simon, we find the width of vision of a genius, for nearly all the not strictly economic theories of the later socialists are contained in his works in embryo, then we find in Fourier a genuine critique, full of French wit but no less deeply penetrating for all that, of the prevailing state of society.[61]

Politics were always in the foreground. Since Quesnay, France has not produced an economist of world renown; in contrast to England which right up to modern times with Keynes has been predominant in this field. From 1789 to 1871, however, France went through four revolutions, world-wide in their consequences, with which no single one in England can compare.

No wonder that in France the political embers continued to glow, whether in the form of small secret societies or of friendly societies and journeymen's associations. Well might an old *montagnard* say that in 1795 the nation had 'come into a state of

A medal cast in memory of the martyrs of 27, 28 and 29 July 1830.

rest'; nevertheless the French nation at rest was politically even more active than many other nations of the time who were strenuously engaged in social struggles.

Only a little more than a third of a century after the entry 'into a state of rest', the people of France gave a new character to revolutionary activity, judged by European standards. Hobsbawm says of it:

The revolutions of 1830 changed the situation entirely. As we have seen, they were the first products of a very general period of acute and widespread economic and social unrest and rapidly quickening social change. Two chief results followed from this. The first was that mass politics and mass revolution on the 1789 model once again became possible and the exclusive reliance on secret brotherhoods therefore less necessary. The Bourbons were overthrown in Paris by a characteristic combination of crisis in what passed for the politics of the Restoration monarchy and popular unrest induced by economic depression. So far from mass inactivity, the Paris of July 1830 showed the barricades springing up in greater number and in more places than ever before or after. (In fact 1830 made the barricade into the symbol of popular insurrection. Though its revolutionary history in Paris goes back to at least 1588, it played no important part in 1789–94.) The second result was that, with the progress of capitalism, 'the people' and 'the labouring poor' – i.e. the men who built barricades – could be increasingly identified with the new industrial proletariat as 'the working class'. A proletarian socialist revolutionary movement therefore came into existence.[62]

Auguste Barbier however saluted the new hero of the revolution thus:

> He is handsome, this giant with broad manly shoulders,
> strong in his rags,
> this noble jobber with his woollen jacket stained
>   with the blood of the enemy!
> This man who shatters thrones with one blow,
> and who, under an oppressive sky,
> sends crowns bouncing over the paving stones like
>   children's hoops!

Recast to correspond with its historical rôle, France's proletariat was appropriating to itself the great legacy of the French Revolution. On 30 April Heine reported from Paris:

'Tell me what you have sown today, and I shall prophesy what harvest you will reap tomorrow.' This proverb by the worthy Sancho came to me as I was thinking of the days when I used to visit one or two studios in the Faubourg Saint Marceau and there discovered what reading matter was being handed round to the *ouvriers*, the most powerful section of the lower classes. It was there that I found several new editions of the speeches of old Robespierre, also of Marat's pamphlets, on production of a few *sous*, Cabet's *History of the Revolution*, Cormenin's poisonous libels, Babeuf's *Doctrine* and Buonarroti's *Conspiracy*, writings which reeked of blood; and I heard songs sung which seemed to have been composed in Hell, and whose choruses gave rise to the wildest excitement. No, it is impossible for anyone in our gentle circle to have the remotest idea of the diabolical sounds which pervaded these songs; one must have heard such as these with one's own ears, for instance, in those vast workshops where metals are forged, and the half-clad, defiant figures beat time during the singing with their great iron hammers on the booming anvils. Such an accompaniment has the most powerful effect, as does the brilliant light when the forge spits forth its angry sparks. Naught but passion and fire!

Now appeared numerous special organs of the labour movement; at their head were the *Journal des Ouvriers*, *Le Peuple* and *L'Artisan*, followed by many, many more: Saint-Simon's *Le Globe*,

Fourier's *Nouveau Monde*, Cabet's *Le Populaire* and *Le Prolétaire Philosophe*.[63]

How vigorously self-aware the working class was now! It was not a Socialist or Communist paper but the *Semeur* of 20 and 27 November 1833, a mouthpiece of 'religious workers', which wrote:

Since the irrevocable victory of the people's cause, the workers have possessed a full awareness of their strength . . . and besides this they have a feeling, though it may not be quite clear, that the bourgeoisie were casting away the banner of the workers, since they (the bourgeoisie) did not need the workers any more to fight against the privileged classes. This is the cause too of the feeling of pride in the working class, the angry suspicion of the upper classes . . .

The years between 1830 and 1848 were filled with risings the like of which were not seen in other countries, neither England nor Germany nor the United States; rebellion by the Paris workers in June 1832 and April 1834, serious riots of the Lyon workers in 1831 and 1834, an insurrection under Blanqui in 1839, disturbances in Lille, Clermont and Toulouse in 1840, great politically-inspired strikes of carpenters and joiners in 1833 and 1845 in Paris, and mineworkers' strikes in Anzin in 1833 and in St Étienne in 1844 and 1846.[64] Quite naturally, along with the word 'socialism' which so often served these movements as a slogan, the word 'internationalism' was already being heard: and most vehemently on the lips of the great Flora Tristan.

And then the revolution of 1848 – with its June days in which the people under the leadership of the proletariat stood alone for the first time in history against a world of enemies, and was so terribly beaten. But the extent of the defeat was kept from the people at the time. Marx, filled with lofty anger and bitter and dignified grief, wrote in the *Neue Rheinische Zeitung* at the end of that month (29 June 1848):

The Paris workers have been suppressed by superior forces, they have not submitted to them. They are beaten, but their opponents are vanquished.

The momentary triumph of brutal power has been bought with the destruction of the delusions and fancies of the February revolution, with the dissolution of the entire old-republican party, with the splitting of the French nation into two nations, the nation of the owners and the nation of the workers. The republic of the *tricoleur* now wears only one colour, the colour of defeat, the colour of blood. It has become the red republic . . .

But the plebeians, tormented by hunger, humiliated by the press, abandoned by doctors, reviled by the respectable as robbers, incendiaries, galley slaves; with their wives and children further plunged into endless misery, the best of those who survive deported overseas – theirs are the dark, threatening brows which it is the privilege and the right of the democratic press to wreathe with the victor's laurel.

But almost four years later, he was compelled to state in the *New York Daily Tribune* (18 March 1852):

The Paris proletariat was beaten, decimated, shattered, to such an extent that up to this very day they have not recovered.

The French working class was the only one at that time mature in its consciousness, and experienced in political warfare.

Slowness of industrial development. Yet how 'naturally' we have traced the reasons for this uniqueness! Everyone will understand the special emphasis on politics, the precociousness, one might say, of class-consciousness in the ideology of the French working class when it has been traced back in this way. But having explained everything so simply, we must point out another special feature apparent in the formation of the French working class, which erects a whole barrier of difficulties in the face of everything we have noted, and represents the development that has been illustrated almost as a miracle.

This feature is the slowness with which the Industrial Revolution proceeded in France, the sluggishness of industrialisation; one might almost say the slow, furtive building-up of a genuine industrial proletariat working with machines. Research into the causes of this development is nothing new. We find them very quickly, and the American researcher, Cameron, enumerates the

most important authors, beginning with Proudhon,[65] proceeding via Lysis[66] as far as Combe,[67] and we can count Cameron[68] himself in with them.

Many of the causes are given here:

The slow increase in population.

An extraordinary polarisation of incomes.

High overseas investments, government loans and private hoarding of gold.

High expenditure on consumer goods and small capital investment.

Emigration of skilled workers and technicians.

Small coal revenues.

Limited public ownership.

A policy of protective customs duty.

A large state bureaucracy.

In so far as these are relevant facts, they undoubtedly played a part, but I do not think that any single one of them had a truly decisive importance. Even Landes,[69] who rebukes French industrialists for a lack of enterprise, fails to hit the nail on the head, any more than the old and often so intelligent Héron de Villefosse, who threw the responsibility on to the 'insatiable monopolists who sacrifice all enterprise for their own speculation'.

I consider the chief reason to have been the victory of the

Manufacture Nationale, Paris, 1800. At the time this was the only steelworks in France that compared with those in Sheffield.

193

peasants in the Great Revolution. This gave a great number of them a small piece of land which they held on to despite their poverty and their debts, which began with the Restoration and continued and increased during the whole of the nineteenth century and later.

Why had England made such rapid progress in the industrialisation of the countryside? Because she had expropriated the peasants, because the peasant had largely disappeared from the English economy when the Industrial Revolution set in.

When Engels wrote as late as 1894:

The peasant has hitherto held his place as a factor of political power mainly because of his apathy, caused by the isolation of country life. This apathy in the majority of the population is the greatest mainstay not only of parliamentary corruption in Paris and Rome, but also of Russian despotism.[70]

This apathy was at work not only in the political field but in the economic and technical field as well, and did not apply to peasants only, but affected all the people around them, including those occupied in handcrafts, retail businesses, and so on.

How angrily the *Haute Banque* spoke out against the thousand and one trivial extortions which were rife under these conditions. The cut-throat discount-brokers and usurers whom Balzac had always portrayed (in contrast with the *Haute Banque*, which he mentioned very little) – Grandet, Gobseck, Métivier and many others – not only played a large rôle in Paris, but were also closely connected with their colleagues in the country. On the other side to them, and clearly separate both socially and in its spheres of interest, was the *Haute Banque*. Even in 1824 Laffitte was writing about economy in the country which was mostly 'at the mercy of ignorance, the daily round and poverty, and in the toils of usury'.[71] In the town, however, particularly in Paris, these circles brought the *Haute Banque* into disrepute – when the latter was merely trying to avoid every little dirty swindle in order to be able to attend to its own big business.

A FAUT ESPERER Q'EU'JEU LA FINIRA BEN TOT

Is it coincidence that the countries of Europe containing most of the peasants, namely England and Germany, had the most rapid industrial expansion? Of course not. Only by a pitiless sacrifice of the peasants was such a process of industrialisation possible. And for this it was not just a case of producing operatives and a corresponding industrial army of reserve. It was also a matter of removing a powerful support of all reactionary forces; and not principally a political, but an economic prop. Everything 'trivial' from the country artisan with his small plot of land to the usury credit-system in the countryside so detested by Laffitte, and the country small-trader, was based on the system of the small holding and with it formed a firm, sluggish element which impeded industrial progress. Marx also made this definition, just as harshly when in his study of the nationalisation of real estate he said:

In France, real estate is open to all who can buy it, but it is just this advantage which brought about the cutting-up of estates into small parcels, to be

SAVOIS BEN QU'JAURIONS NOT TOUR.

A double cartoon representing the change wrought in the condition of French peasants by the Renunciations of 4 August 1789.

cultivated by men who possessed only scanty means and were dependent on their own physical labour and that of their families. This form of land-ownership, involving the cultivation of fragments of land, not only excludes the employment of modern agricultural improvements, but at the same time makes the countryman himself the most headstrong opponent of any social progress and above all of the nationalisation of real estate.[72]

It made the small French peasant the most headstrong opponent of any social progress!

There was of course a 'genuine proletariat' in the textile industry. But how powerful still were hand-crafts! How important hand-work was compared with machine-work in the same industry! As late as 1830 there were eighty thousand outworkers and craft-workers in the cotton industry compared with fifty-five thousand factory-workers. And if in 1851 for every entrepreneur in the textile industry of the *département* Seine-Inférieure there were three hundred and thirty workers, in no other *département* were there as many as thirty-five, and in the Seine *département* there were only ten.[73]

Next to agriculture and in conjunction with it (both outside the cities and even in them, in the suburbs), craft-work decided the way of life of the majority of employees. The situation in about 1810, when in England the great wave of machine-breaking was about to descend, is assessed thus by Sée[74]:

As the craft industry predominated, close-knit groups of workers did not yet exist except in Paris and a few cities. The labour movement was not a factor with which Napoleon had to reckon.

On the situation one generation later, he remarks[75]:

The fact that industrial freedom was achieved in a period when craft-work still held the upper hand enabled it to be adapted in time to economic changes and to limit itself to its own special sphere of operation. This sphere was quite wide enough, for there was among producers and consumers alike an innate appreciation – furthered by Colbertism – of solid workmanship and good quality which guaranteed it a market far beyond national boundaries for high-class household equipment, the clothing of a financially sound clientèle, and for artistic or luxury goods.

And when he touches on the poor conditions for factory workers during this period, he concludes by saying:

But these defects were to be found only in heavy industry and one must guard against making generalisations. Not only because the main working force was still generally speaking on the land, but also because heavy industry formed only a narrow class within the world of trade, for craft work had continued to be very widespread.[76,77]

Under these conditions an hereditary proletariat was able to evolve, particularly in textile towns, which existed in France just as in England or the United States. At the same time the number of 'authentic working men's families' was still relatively small even in 1850. There was certainly a violent aversion among countryfolk to 'mixing' their families with those of factory workers. However the attitude of the artisans, an extraordinarily heterogeneous group, was different.

Sée is right to refer to the existence of a considerable luxury trade, employing large numbers, and of high quality, the only one of its kind in the entire world of capitalist labour (it was exceeded in scope and to some extent in quality by Chinese and Indian manufacture). In addition, there was a thriving manufacture of a lower quality intended to satisfy day-to-day needs. It was to some degree linked closely with home industry, which in its turn was closely connected with domestic outwork. The difference between these last two was that domestic outwork employed only members of the same family and rarely worked for the market direct. Nevertheless the artisans concerned in this manufacture were closely connected with the factory proletariat, not right from the beginning, but more and more as time went on.

Sometimes one is in a dilemma how to define the social position of the parties in question. We have mentioned the riots in Lyon. The silk-weavers of this town rose for the first time in the thirties, on 21 November 1831. On the twenty-third the town was in their hands. Only after the bitterest battles was the rising, that historic rehearsal for the Commune of 1871, put down, but then only through the armed might of twenty thousand soldiers supported by fifty guns. In February 1834 the Lyon silk workers rose again. Thirty thousand workers fought for eleven days, from 14 to 24 February, against a lowering of wages. In vain. On 9 April the battle was resumed. Barricades arose in the streets and divided the people more sharply than ever. This rebellion by the tormented heroes of the Lyon silk factories went on for four whole days. The general in command of government forces gave the order: 'All of them must be killed. Comrades – have no pity! Be merciless . . . We must bring about a slaughter in which three thousand rebels shall perish!' The rebellion was crushed.

There follows a brief note about the organisation of the Lyon silk industry:

In reality the production of silk required the intervention of three different economic elements: the factory owners who supplied the raw materials, who numbered about eight-hundred; the shop-masters, approximately ten

thousand of them, who on an average owned five looms each and kept part of the wages for themselves, and finally thirty to forty thousand workers. Masters and workers, in spite of their seemingly contrary interests often made common cause together. Joint friendly societies (there were eight of them) had been set up under the Empire and the Restoration.[78]

Were those who numbered from three to four in one business really modern industrial workers? But they worked with machines and represented an enormous concentration of labour. And what about the masters and the artisans? At all events they were displaced artisans, who were not independent and, even if the machines were their own property, they did not buy the raw materials.

And this remarkable proletariat, this remarkable element of the working class, was born in riots and is rightly referred to as the forerunner of the Commune. In riots of which the first was completely unpolitical in intent, Sée's account of the rising of 1831 was:

As Eugen Tarle has pointed out, it was merely a hunger march without any political overtones. But it became the starting point of constant economic and even political unrest. Whereas the workers in the July Revolution appeared in the train of the bourgeoisie, one year later they were bold

Insurrection at Lyon: the battle of Pont Morand,
November 1831. In 1831 and again in 1834, the
Lyon silk-weavers rioted in protest against the
lowering of wages.

199

enough to mount an attack on their own, and, for the first time, with their own resources.[79,80]

We have enlarged upon two features of the French working class, namely: first the exceedingly rapid and powerful political development, which can be most clearly measured by the swift maturing of its class-consciousness, in a society glutted with revolutionary tradition, and whose eminent historians, true children of the bourgeois community, evolved the theory of the class struggle, the theory of history as a history of class struggles, long before Marx; secondly the exceedingly slow industrial development (in a society where the peasant and the artisan played a relatively large part) with its corresponding effect on the rate of growth of a modern industrial proletariat.

These two special features hang closely together, in the same degree as they appear to be inconsistent. We have only to consider the Lyon silk-weavers, who may be said, with certain qualifications, to represent the modern industrial proletariat. But there can be no doubt that they were genuine sons and grandsons of the *Grande Révolution* – genuine both in a genealogical and an ideological sense. While the artisan influence in Germany was mainly counter-revolutionary, if not reactionary, its effect in France was revolutionary; and yet the small artisans and traders had formed the hard core of Robespierre's regime.

Germany: industrial revolution in a semi-feudal society

As early as 1829 Goethe was writing in *Reflections and Thoughts of Journeymen*:

The stifling of steam-engines is as impossible from a practical as from a moral point of view. An active trade, the rustle of paper money, the mounting debts to pay more debts: these are all enormous factors with which the young man of today is faced. Happy is he if he is endowed by nature with a sober and quiet mind to prevent his making unreasonable demands on the world and allowing his destiny to be dictated by it.[81]

Machines could not be suppressed but they were only one of the numerous factors which could confuse a young man. Apart from machines, the other factors were, in purely commercial terms – trade, paper money and debts – all of which England had experienced in the sixteenth century. In addition to this, and it was not unnatural in a poet who saw himself threatened by a philistine capitalism (in contrast with the art-loving age of feudalism!) his whole outlook was pervaded by unrest and a rejection of the too impetuous forward march of the forces of production; all positive feelings of joy and steady optimism towards the new age just beginning were absent, and so even the 'Olympian security and peace' of the later Goethe could not influence his views on the Industrial Revolution.

The hero in Immerman's novel *Die Epigonen* says of the situation in Germany:

It would be a sad day for me if I ever wanted anything in Germany . . . It is as if in our fume-ridden atmosphere a decision could only be arrived at, but certainly not carried out. But just because I do not want anything else, I am nowhere more at home than in Germany . . . Without an aim or a goal the hours must pass me by, for aim is only another word for folly, and if one sets oneself a goal, one can be quite certain of being dragged in the opposite direction by the whirlpool of circumstances.[82]

Hoesch steelworks, 1838. In Germany the
transition period between feudalism and industrialism
was keenly felt about sixty years after
industrial capitalism was established in England.

201

Everywhere there was dissension, insecurity, transition, and thus we find men everywhere who had not 'found' themselves, partly because they could not, partly because they would not, and Immerman, the most important novelist of this period, makes us feel this acutely, without however being entirely exact in his details, but nevertheless imparting the atmosphere in a stark and terrifying way:

Of course the core of the nobility has rotted away, but the hard outer casing still stands and one can go on cracking one's head against it.[83]

'We are of course living in a transitional period,' said Wilhelmi. This word has become banal, and all schoolboys bandy it about. It is not so easy to appreciate its full import, to take really to heart how many men are sacrificed to this sort of transition.[84]

Among men who were sacrificed to this sort of transition were not by any means only people such as feudal dukes, but also workers, formerly at work on the land and now driven into a factory by the Industrial Revolution:

What was horrifying was the sickly pallor of the workers' faces. That second estate could be picked out from those who had remained true to the soil by the fact that its members had, whether near the furnace, in the midst of the iron ore or at the weaving-loom, not only implanted the germ of death in themselves, but had done the same for their children also; the latter, pale and bloated, crept around among the highways and by-ways. Hermann often saw in boldest relief the effect of the two occupations, the one natural, the other artificial, on people. While he saw behind ploughs faces which brimmed over with good health, he was aware of others at machines with sunken cheeks and hollow eyes, whose family likeness enabled one to recognise them as brothers or cousins of the healthy ones.[85]

The second reason for my trip to Germany was that I wanted to engage another good servant. I had had to dismiss my previous one, who meant well but stood around the whole time doing nothing. As the party most concerned, I thought I could put my foot down, but since freedom of trade was universal, I could do nothing about it: any lout could mean well. I wanted to obtain a replacement for my servant only from Germany, for every country has its own special products which one cannot obtain elsewhere in the same excellence. Spain has its wines, Italy its songs, England its constitution, Russia its Muscovy hides, France has the Revolution and in Germany the servants turn out to be the best.[86]

That is the genuine, bitterly satirical Immerman, friend of Heine, and it is not surprising that it not only hints at the nobility, which is shown up in a ludicrous light, but the people also.

So much for the writers.

In 1816, Ottfried Müller, a young man who was later to be a star in the firmament of scholarship, came to Berlin to do research in Greek antiquity and wrote to a friend:

I am now sitting here in the foulest and most worthless of all cities, which a true and patriotically-minded Silesian should scarcely set foot in, let alone contemplate; I am here in wretched Berlin, which is beneath contempt and beggars description. The Court presses down like a lead weight on all classes and squashes all who strive to soar into the heights, when their wings perhaps ought not yet to be clipped. By this means it keeps everyone in the confines of a police state and a culture beyond all bounds and it revels delightedly about the marvellous prosperity of a very fine, elegant and conventional civilisation. Hence the misery and beggarliness which lie imprinted on the deeply furrowed brows of all Berliners; and in public gardens – if there could be said to be any here – and on leisurely strolls, there is nothing so rare as a loud, happy, joyful Silesian laugh. It is the same for all classes here. And now for the University – God be merciful to us![87]

In 1824 the widow of the scholar Georg Forster warned her daughter in these terms – she confessed this to a friend: 'I wrote to my daughter who is pregnant again; I told her she was not to bear me a grandchild, for we need no more sons.'[88] In 1841, however, Alexander von Humboldt wrote: 'It has become a deplorable age, in which Germany has dropped a long way behind England and France.'[89] So much for the scholastic community; about which the King of Hanover remarked: 'Professors, tarts and ballerinas are two a penny.'[90]

In the archives of the principal businessman and industrialist from the Rhineland, Harkort, his biographer found two letters

The structure of German society, from *Kladderadatsch*, 1849: 'The proletarian is exploited by the bourgeoisie, the bourgeoisie is oppressed by the nobility; in this way the pyramid of the state is maintained . . .' On the top is Frederick William IV, King of Prussia.

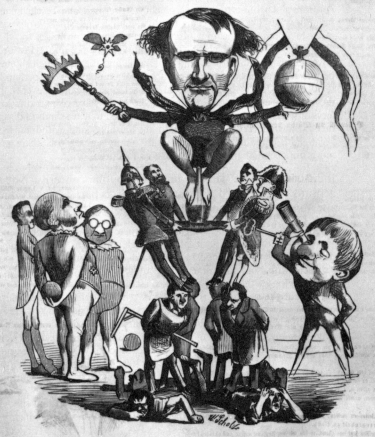

184

Japanische Tändeleien nach Rappo,

oder

wie die Lasten des Staates gleichmäßig vertheilt sind, um die Krone balanciren zu können.

Der Proletarier vom Bürger gequetscht, der Bürger vom Adel belästigt,
So wird die Pyramide des Staats gegipfelt und schlau befestigt.
So zeiget ein Jeder auf Höhern Befehl der Kraft und Balance Proben,
Getreu dem alten Naturgesetz: der Druck kommt stets von Oben!

from a friend in 1816, telling him about the situation:

Anything that was planned or that happened in Berlin was not experienced by the population; the newspapers gave little information about state affairs and the only thing of which the citizens were given detailed reports were the finance minister von Bulow's measures, which could be condensed into one sentence: the old taxes were as before and new ones were added. Petitions and protests to the government were refused, and Teschenmacher's[91] opinion was: 'They are fleecing us alive.' Our friend Stuck wrote with mild sarcasm about the meaningless words and empty promises to which the people were being subjected. The nobility was once more favoured, the government was nurturing feelings of caste, and the sun which shone on the people had rapidly clouded over, if not set completely . . . perhaps it was really better to lay one's hands in one's lap and wait on events, but the individual could change nothing and the great wave of patriotic love and fervour which had seized the people had receded to leave sands of disappointment. Slowly everyone returned to his business and withdrew from the great state community into the small family circle. Was there anything more important than children and grandchildren?[92]

Industrialists were withdrawing from public concerns. Not so the artisans, who played a particularly large part in the community and town life. Heinrich Simon remarked in his journal in 1836:

I had an audience of the Minister of Justice and took occasion to tell him the plain truth about the legal and other conditions in New Pomerania. The situation was too shocking for words. New Pomerania was most dissatisfied with the government and quite rightly so. The guild system had developed there and continued steadily in a way almost without parallel in the rest of Germany. Laws which applied to the culture and industrial activity of the sixteenth century were supposed to suit present-day conditions. For instance, when silk hats first appeared and a dealer in them ordered some, a hatter brought an action against him because they were hats. It was contended that they consisted of cardboard with a silk covering, that is to say, material quite foreign to a hatter. A book-binder seized hold of this and gave his opinion that the cardboard work was the main thing, the covering only secondary; it was his business to deal with this commodity. When a new sort of comfortable slipper appeared, slipper- and shoe-makers immediately attacked one another and the question arose, which was the essential part of a slipper, and which of the shoe? Next, all sorts of slippers were produced and the judge had to decide about them; and so it went on.[93]

Under these conditions, capital and labour combined for a while against semi-feudalism. The following is a report on the building of a mechanical cotton-spinning and weaving mill in Augsburg at the end of the thirties:

In this former imperial city one is constantly seeing the influence of traditions handed down from the ancient period of craft guilds, in spite of the French Revolution and the fact that the city had been part of the Kingdom of Bavaria for more than thirty years. It was no longer a question of rebellion and riotous mobs, but attempts were made in those circles which always hoped for a return to the 'good old days' to make life as hard as possible for the new developments outside the Jakobertor (James Gate). The new developments were that an 'anonymous' company was engaging artisans to put up a building. The question was therefore being asked, how this was to be arranged. The association of journeyman-masons raised an objection that all journeyman-masons or foremen would have to join the association and pay registration fee and subscriptions. The Catholic journeymen demanded additional contributions to the guild's banner, but the masons resisted this; they intended naturally to pay the subscriptions, but registration fees and contributions towards a banner were unreasonable demands to their way of thinking. As they declared that they would rather leave the site than pay these expenses, the situation was made more critical than at first appeared. The magistrate had also threatened the directors with coercive measures if they did not collect the required amount of duty within a week. The manager protested against this, saying that it was not within the duties of a contractor to collect the city taxes. This was admitted by the magistrate, but he pointed out that they had wanted to avoid presenting summonses to individual journeymen and thereby use this roundabout way via the management to pay what was in itself a not very large amount from their own pockets, in order to let the matter drop. Doubtless this solution would have been simpler for the manager, but as he foresaw quite rightly that it might incite people to act in a similar way in the future, he did not take this step. He informed the workers of the demands and had their opposition recorded by the building engineering manager Kraemer in a comprehensive report, which he then sent to the magistrate with the request to have a government decision upon it. The affair was settled when the association of journeymen-masons was abolished forthwith.[94]

The most important reason for semi-feudalism in Germany (and in the more progressive regions of Eastern Europe) was the method of transition from feudalism to capitalism in agriculture. Agriculture was the main economic basis of feudalism. Land-owners and farmers were the main classes of feudal society.

For one reason or another – the Wars of the Roses, the English Revolution of 1642, the French Revolution of 1789 – the over-whelming majority of feudal lords in the country disappeared in England and France. In their place stepped new landowners with their capitalistic economic methods: in other words, peasant-proprietors. But in Germany the transition was slow and it left the old feudal lords in possession of their land and also in their positions in the state administration and the army, in accordance with feudal custom, and only drove them gradually to start managing their land on capitalist lines.

In these circumstances the peasants were certainly free to give up their land, their smallholding, to present it to the owner and move into the town, or they were forced to purchase their land by paying instalments to the owner, and by numerous feudal disburse-ments, such as ground-rent, money in kind in the form of spinning, poultry, watchman's duties, eggs, sweeping, chimney-sweeping or bodyguard, additional heavy labour, harvesting and other such payments.

But when the country was still semi-feudal and the land-owners were in charge of national administration, then quite naturally the petty bourgeoisie, artisans and tradesmen alike, found support in the semi-feudal authorities. In a garrison town, with officers of noble rank, the shoe-makers, restaurateurs, glovers and small money-lenders saw in them the pinnacles of society, with whom they might converse 'directly'. In the assize cities, there were tailors, book-sellers and others who had 'direct contact' with semi-feudal society life.

If one takes into account the hatred shared by feudal nobility and artisans for their competitors, the industrialists and workers, then the bond uniting them was not only the memory of the 'good old feudal days', when everyone had his rightful place, not merely the relationship of the petty bourgeoisie to the semi-feudal authorities (an economically dependent relationship nevertheless, which provided employment), but also the common revulsion, well-founded economically-speaking, against the new age, against 'barefaced' capitalism and 'industrialism'.

The feudal element was still so strong that at times the workers even used it as a weapon against the capitalists. We find workers who even directed these feudal elements against the capitalists in those districts where there was no longer any obligation to join a guild, but in which the spirit of the guilds was still very much preserved in the form of certain specific mutual-assistance organisations. When, in 1845, machinery was to be introduced into the Berlin calico-printing works, incorporating devices for laying the printing-dyes on the cloth, the employers were on the point of replacing skilled workers by apprentices. The calico-printers were powerful enough to prevent this, and the ministers Bodelschwingh and Flottwell wrote to the King on 11 May 1846:

The greatest obstacle, however, seems to lie in the corporate spirit among the calico-printers, which unites them and is linked with a certain pride in skills they have acquired. From this alone one can account for the fact that they are attempting, by inadmissible methods and all kinds of chicanery, to persuade those of their number who are changing over to working with machines at the request of the factory owners, not to do so.[95]

The feudal element was still so strong that entire social strata, which in England and France could be counted as the working class in the broadest sense, had to be locked out in Germany until 1850. This was especially true of the mine-workers, who, it must be admitted, had a labour discipline – indeed, a discipline of life – which recalled feudal conditions. Thus there were regions, even in Prussia, in which pitmen under a certain age could only get married with the permission of the mining authorities. Lärmer,[96] for instance, gives the following account of the Mansfeld district:

In the 1828 records of the Eisleben mine-office the following minute appears; it is one of many:

'Apprentice miner Gottlieb Erdmeyer of Blankenheim, aged twenty one and a half, who, according to his own deposition, has put Amalie Kegel with child out of wedlock, is willing to marry the said woman, and accordingly hereby requests the royal worshipful mining-board for the necessary marriage licence.'[97]

This motion was not signed by Erdmeyer himself, but by three officials. Nevertheless, the mining board made the following resolution:

'For putting Amalie Kegel with child out of wedlock, apprentice miner Gottlieb Erdmeyer of Blankenheim has been expelled from the apprentice mining class and condemned to drive horses, and this is hereby recorded as a supplement to the records.'[98]

There was no question of the grant of a marriage licence. Meanwhile it must not be forgotten that the legal stipulations (General Civil Code) entitled any man who reached the age of eighteen to contract a marriage. However, the Prussian mining office waged an energetic battle to prevent miners from marrying before their twenty-fourth year, as had been laid down in general terms in the incorporated miners' constitution. They were able to fight this successfully because the General Civil Code gave the opportunity of forbidding a contract of marriage if the necessary income to feed a family was not guaranteed. It was not difficult for the mining-offices to produce such evidence, since young mine-workers did not, as a rule, become pitmen until they were twenty-four. But just let us study the arguments of a few Prussian mining officials on the qualifications for and necessity of granting a marriage licence to the mine-workers. The Rothenberg mining office, in a letter dated September 26th 1789, put the point of view that the refusal of marriage licences to older miners made it impossible for the latter to marry young women, for these would be thrown with their children on to the mercy of the miners' provident fund in the event of the miner's death.[99]

Other mining offices felt that marriage licences should be prepared, 'for the sake of order'; 'to prevent people getting married when young and impecunious'; 'because this is how it has always been done'; also, because the transfer of miners to other districts would be complicated; and so on. The ministers responsible for spiritual, educational and medical affairs; of the interior; and also of trade, industry and mines put the following point of view regarding this question in a joint memorandum to the Prussian king on May 10th 1833:

The continuance of this stipulation [i.e. the obtaining of a marriage licence – J.K.] is necessary and desirable, not only by reason of the indispensable income for the miners' provident fund brought in in this way, but also from the point of view of the police, to keep the register of miners in order.'[100]

On 29 January 1849, the Kamsdorf mining office defended its attitude as follows:

Because people cannot become pitmen before their twenty-fourth birthday, they would not, in their earlier employment as labourers or apprentice miners, be able to maintain a family on their pay; they would lose their strength through worry and bad food; they would not be able to hold down their jobs competently, and, dying early, they and their families would be a burden on the miners' provident fund.[101]

Often this feudal 'discipline of life' was inseparable from military discipline. The young mine-workers, pitmen and boys, were forced to wear uniform even on the way to and from work.

In addition, special instructions were issued about turn-out, and regulations for saluting were made which scarcely differed from army rules, even in the way they were carried out.

In the pit they went on using the simple phrase 'good luck!' Outside the pit, however, the miners had to observe the following rules:

When off duty, all miners and boys must, as soon as they meet a mining official whom they can easily recognise by his uniform, or as soon as he comes past, stand still, or, if walking, look him in the face, at the same time greeting him with "good luck!" and remove any headgear they may be wearing, but to refrain completely from all other forms of salutation, such as a bow. The uniform pit-helmet, however, will not be removed, but the latter may only be worn with full uniform of the correct pattern. A man dressed thus must, as before, only when he meets a uniformed official, turn and face him in full military fashion, and stand still until the official has passed.'[102]

How he should greet his superiors had been explained to every single man in this way. The workers were shown how the officials should be greeted when they were standing together in larger groups. To the relevant passage of item three of the order was added:

Ladder shaft in the Harz mines, Germany. Whereas in most other countries miners could be included in the working class by 1850, in Germany they still had feudal obligations to their employers: they had to wear uniforms and salute their superiors, and were subject to harsh militaristic discipline.

'The customary gatherings and groups in conversation, which assemble on the roadway and outside houses, particularly on pay-days, will not be prohibited, but this must not lead to the omission of greetings.

In this case the member of the group who first sees an official approaching must inform his colleagues so that all of them may greet in the manner prescribed in item two.'[103]

In addition to the foremen and sifters, the oldest miners themselves were also responsible for the implementation of these directions, and so the authorities used this measure to appraise the miners' *esprit de corps*.

All this does not exclude the fact that this discipline was clearly a discipline of compulsion, and, for the mining boys, a discipline by the rod. Any infringement of the regulations for greetings was, in the first instance, punished by a pay stoppage of one *groschen*, and on subsequent occasions by piecework rates and demotion, that is, assignment to harder and worse-paid work. Mining boys received instead from four to sixteen lashes with the rope.

In order to achieve a deterrent effect, beatings were administered in the presence of the entire work force immediately after prayers and before the pit descent. On the third infringement, the miners were laid off for specific or indefinite periods.[104]

What a great deal these measures achieved!

All miners under twenty-four could be paid the lowest wages, as they were not allowed to marry, while, by forbidding the marriages of older miners to young women, one protected the provident fund from long-term payments of widows' pensions. At the same time every miner, on the occasion of his marriage, had to contribute a large sum to the fund (to obtain his marriage licence), and so helped to keep it full.

As far as military discipline was concerned, it gave rise to arbitrary punishment and made it possible, as Immermann would say, to attract ideal employees; on the other hand, it divided the work force into young workers and informers, who were selected from older men.

One can see how bureaucratic semi-feudalism penetrated so deeply into the productive processes that it also determined the structure of the operatives' grades. And, in this case, the resul

was to make it impossible to include the mine-workers in the modern industrial proletariat, during the period of the Industrial Revolution up to 1850.

The feudal element was so strong that in the Germany of this period even the workers on the land could not be confidently included in the working class. In 1830 there was a report in England on the land; it concerned machine-breaking directed against the introduction of threshing-machines, and mass strikes in which nine workers were hanged and four hundred and fifty sent to the colonies as convicts. Those are the modern workers here referred to. In France, where the number of workers on the land was relatively small, one might have doubts whether to include them in the working class. One can be quite certain that in Germany such an inclusion was quite out of the question. The land-workers in Germany were maids, manservants and jobbing labourers, of whom the latter frequently owned a small piece of land. This tied them firmly to the locality and to the landowner. Paul quotes a memorandum from

the day wage-labourers at Wusterbach to the Prussian king on April 23rd 1848. In this memorandum they pointed out that they were being over-burdened by their landlord Wittnow, a tenant-farmer, with compulsory service to the lord of the manor, and other manual labour; and that they received little pay and had excessive working hours, for they had to work from six in the morning until dark, and in summer sometimes even during the night when there was a full moon. They were under such a strong obligation to do this work that if they refused, they lived in fear of being given notice to quit their lodgings and of having to leave the village. This they did not wish to do, as the majority of them had been born and bred in it.[105]

The manservants and maids, however, came under the regulations for servants which were completely patriarchal in character and enabled the 'master' to punish the maid, and forbade the manservant to give notice if he had not 'served his time' (which was of many years' duration). They also subjected young people who did this work, even if they did not wear a uniform like the young miners, to a discipline which was little different from that practised in feudal times on the mill-workers in their barracks: everything, from eating to church-going and marriage, was controlled by the 'master'.

In other words, the working class in Germany during the period under review was still relatively small, as whole groups of workers which in England and France formed part of it were missing. Also, they began their development two generations later than in England and one generation later than in France, since important feudal ties did not fall away until much later, between 1805 and 1810.

One might think, perhaps, that the working class in Germany also differed from those in other countries in that they stood isolated from associated grades, for instance, from lesser trades, since these continued to be bound by many feudal ties (to some extent there was still a purely feudal obligation to join a guild) and were ideologically associated with the semi-feudal grades of the ruling classes. But there can be no question of this; the trades and the working class were similar but not for the same reasons as in France. Whereas the revolutionary tradition linked poor mechanical trades with the working class in France, it was the reverse in Germany, where the close atmosphere of semi-feudalism caused History to be 'short of breath' as it advanced into a new age. A considerable portion of the working class existed in the stuffy atmosphere of semi-feudalism which enveloped all employees and they were not yet recognisable as a class, until extreme poverty and the excessive use of arbitrary powers caused movements which enabled the veil to be lifted from their eyes. At the end of the period under consideration there was definitely an hereditary proletariat but on a smaller scale than in France. The number of 'genuine proletarian families' was still small; but it was the workers' families which continued to be overwhelmingly large; nevertheless, there was in these at least one grandparent or brother or sister (by marriage, at any rate) or children too who belonged to other classes, the peasantry or small-holding day-labourers, tradesmen, house servants or small business concerns.

The railway navvies. In a country with a working class structure of this kind, one group stood out in complete isolation as soon as it appeared: the railway 'navvies'.

What sort of workers were they? Eichholtz, who studied them closely, describes them as follows[106]:

Railway construction was a vast and really important undertaking, performed by many thousands of workers. These cleared huge stretches of land, built embankments, blew up rocks and cliffs, levelled, flattened, and so on.

Never before 1848 were there such gigantic armies of workers in Germany as on the railways. On the longer stretches, many thousands were at work: on the Thuringian railway, for example, there were as many as fifteen thousand workers. Although these workers were for the most part still half proletarian, and though they withdrew to their own villages at harvest time, or at any rate during the winter, to work on their own plots or on their landlord's estate; whichever the case, when railways were being built, the *grande bourgeoisie* was on one side, and (for those days) enormous armies of workers on the other.

When a railway was being built, numerous workers streamed in from the neighbourhood: for instance, day-labourers from the land, domestic workers from the textile trade, craft apprentices, unemployed factory workers. Most labourers engaged in railway construction were itinerant. They often came great distances, and had for many years been moving from one track to another wherever there was work to be had and money to be earned. . . . By way of illustration, seasonal workers from Silesia were already at work in 1835 on the Düsseldorf-Elberfeld railway. Hence the workers on the railways were to a large extent breaking through the narrow frontiers which the German system of small states had erected. Here among the railway 'navvies', proletarian unity was beginning to be a reality, extending over the frontiers of individual German states and even beyond the frontiers of Germany herself.

In the main, the workers, like the mine-workers, lived a primitive social life, isolated from the 'rest of the community', often all together in hastily built barracks; and they were united in the face of both the inclemencies of the weather and the whiplash of the foreman, who was called the gang-master, and who, as contractor to the community, was responsible for the work of gangs comprising one hundred to one hundred and twenty workers.

In many ways one is reminded of the 'wild west', of the gold, silver or copper towns, which suddenly appeared and quickly disappeared again, with their hordes of harlots, gambling-dens, throat-cutting and bank robberies. In Germany a 'town' of this sort spread slowly along a railway track; its existence was even less secure and the people were correspondingly more displaced.

At the same time, this kind of work and style of living was in strong contrast with the semi-feudalistic existence of so many other workers; it brought freshness, independence and a spirit of enterprise; one might almost say it produced unadulterated, pure conditions within production; unmixed with misery and the harsh left-overs of the past, the remains of yesterday's meal in the perspective of history.

Their ideology too matured more quickly in proportion. Wilhelm Wolff had conversations with some of them and wrote a report in the Paris *En Avant*.[107] He observed that he was 'quite astonished at the clear grasp of our social conditions, of the origins of these conditions, and of the principle of a new order of things'. And then he quoted the railway 'navvies':

So long as we work here, we are, it is true, earning our living, but we are well aware that we are only slaving away for the monied classes. The latter do a good bargain with the sweat of our brows, and when the track is laid, we may return whence we came. If we are ill and weak, we may lie down and chew potatoes – if there are any – or die on a dung-heap for all the rich man cares. But there is one advantage in all this for us. We have flocked together in our thousands, we have come to know one another, and in the whole long business of give and take, most of us have become more sensible. There are only very few of us left who believe in the old trumpery. We have now damned little respect for the 'swells' and the rich. What we scarcely even dared to think about in the privacy of our homes, we now air freely among ourselves, namely, that we are the real supporters of the wealthy, we need only to be unwilling to work, and they will be compelled to beg us for their bread and butter or starve, unless they are willing to work themselves. They may think that if the weavers had only held out longer we should soon have become restless. The weavers' cause is basically our cause; and since there are twenty thousand of us working on the Silesian railways, we should certainly have had our say.

The weavers referred to were domestic weavers, who rose in revolt against the obstructive mill-owners in 1844. These weavers were living in the most terrible poverty. Gerhard Hauptmann later dedicated a play to them, and a whole series of contemporary novelists described their condition. Just as Wolff emphasised the ideological maturity of the railway 'navvies', so Marx extolled the weavers' insight into social conditions.

What a strange and 'unclassical' country that Germany of the 1840s was! In it, railway workers and domestic weavers, who worked without machinery, formed the ideological vanguard of the working class.

Other lands, other ages, other types

If we add to those countries which have been discussed Belgium, Holland, Denmark, Sweden, Norway, Austria, Moravia, Hungary, and parts of Northern Italy, we have included the entire group of countries in which what we call an industrial revolution took place. And in none of the countries or parts of countries which we have added to the list is there an evolution to be seen which differs markedly from the examples already given. But whereas we cannot speak of an industrial revolution, of the kind that existed in the four countries discussed above, nevertheless in countries such as Russia, Australia and India – to name but three, each of which had a completely different development from the others – it is clear that a working class was formed.

Russia

Let us take one of the many stories of Russia written in the last thirty years and read about the situation there at the turn of the twentieth century:

Caricature by Doré of Russian nobility who 'changent leur enjeu et jouent leurs biens en terre, et par suite leurs biens en chair.' The remains of serfdom survived in Russia into the twentieth century.

At the beginning of the twentieth century the imperialist system had already spread throughout the world.

In Russia, capitalism developed and grew into imperialism in exactly the same way. But imperialism in Russia had a very special character. Lenin and Stalin called it a militaristic-feudal imperialism. Such an imperialism is one which had all the features of the imperialist system: increased concentration of production, formation of monopolies, export of capital, merging of bank capital with industrial capital, struggle for the division and new distribution of world areas, and the keenest sharpening of class differences. Hence militaristic-feudal imperialism in Russia was in the first place part of the imperialist world-system.

The special feature of imperialism in Tsarist Russia was that innumerable feudal relics still formed part of it. The remains of serfdom had been maintained in industry and agriculture and affected the development both of individual classes and of the entire social and national organisation of Russia in the twentieth century.[108]

Thus we can see a mixture of semi-feudal conditions with the most up-to-date monopolistic methods. Workers in the Putilov works or the Siemens subsidiaries were naturally the same sort of workers as were to be found in Berlin, Paris or London; working perhaps slightly longer hours than those in the west and somewhat worse-paid, but entirely different, and enjoying far better working conditions than the workers in England, New England, France or Prussia around 1840; and by comparison, veritable intellectual giants in their ideological maturity. One might well ask why they are mentioned in this book.

Yet they must be mentioned: as contemporaries of other workers who were working under exactly the same conditions as existed in England one hundred years before; as contemporaries of Russian workers who flocked in their hordes from the country-side to form the work-force of industrial concerns in some provincial town, and who were just beginning to form themselves into a working class, as immature as the workers in 1820 Germany, and perhaps even working with machines of the type used by the great-grandfathers of workers employed in the west.

In other words, we have in Russia a heterogeneous collection of workers' groups in a stage of national development as a class of a completely different type from those in western and central Europe during the Industrial Revolution. We have a heterogeneous collection of types of employees, which correspond to what would emerge if we telescoped and combined several stages of the development of the working classes in Western Europe. That is to say, we have a 'juxtaposition', and not so very infrequently, a 'conjunction' of workers in the same town, who worked sixteen hours a day, with limited productivity, who were mostly illiterate and a long way from any trade-union organisation, but quite ready to destroy machines; and workers who were only employed for ten hours a day, with the most up-to-date machinery, not only organised in trade-unions but politically as well, eagerly reading their morning paper each day.

In addition (and here we are dealing with an attitude which was naturally impossible at the time of the Industrial Revolution), these workers were perhaps thinking that it would be a good thing to acquaint workers employed in conditions similar to those during the Industrial Revolution with the modern ideas of the socialist labour-movement, and win them over to socialism. Or, and this could happen too, they were even scornful of workers employed under such backward conditions, haughtily looking down on them and disowning them as fellow-combatants. These suggestions of the basically different situation in which a working class in Tsarist Russia found itself are sufficient to show that we are dealing here with an evolution which cannot be compared with those discussed on previous pages.

Australia

We shall now take a look at Australia. Colonisation did not begin until 1788, when some thousand men under Captain Phillip were transported to Sydney harbour. Around the middle of the nineteenth century the population numbered about four hundred thousand, to which must be added an unknown number of aboriginals. In the first period of the colonisation of Australia, the white population consisted mainly of convicted people, the majority of whom were criminals; in contrast with the settlers in England's American colonies in the seventeenth and eighteenth centuries.[109] Most of them had been sentenced to seven years penal servitude, in many cases for trivial offences, and some had already served a portion of their sentences in England, so that in quite a short time the majority of the population consisted of people who were free, frequently after serving time. Many of these former convicts quickly took regular, even respectable, jobs, and in early times the colonial government tended to play off these emancipists against the 'arrogant' settlers who had always been free, by giving them preferential treatment.[110]

As there was no land monopoly (the virtual absence of industry caused the movement between professions to be extraordinarily

vigorous), we are presented until well into the first half of the nineteenth century with a society in Australia in which there were the beginnings of class formation, and outlines of classes. Naturally officials sent over to govern belonged to a class in England, just as English capitalists who invested in Australia did; but there can be no question of a division into set classes such as are to be found under capitalism (and naturally there were no classes within progressive social divisions). Australia was not, of course, up to about 1850, a classless society in the sense that there was really no foundation on which to base classes. One should say rather that the foundations were not yet ready for well-defined classes, owing to a large number of special historical circumstances.[111]

Here was a country under capitalist control, in which for sixty years, no classes could be formed at all, since any more solid development was hindered by an extraordinary mobility in every direction. And then, around the middle of the century, the copper- and gold-strikes began.

When gold was first discovered, almost every man rushed to the gold-fields, and there was no need of any capital to strike gold.

German emigrants bound for Australia.
The attraction of Australia was similar to
that of the U.S.A., especially after the
discovery of copper and gold.

221

So many men hurried out to the gold-fields, including officials and policemen, that the Melbourne of 1851 was rightly described as a city of women and children. Elsewhere the situation was similar.

Whenever a new and rich gold-field was discovered, anyone could at first go and extract the gold, for it was lying around to be picked up; but this method of collecting gold quickly came to an end in each case. Real mining operations became necessary, and that meant that the 'small man' was put in a hopeless position, and that it was now only the capitalist with machines and tools who could exploit the gold-field concerned. 'The miner replaced the digger' was Murphy's remark.[112] Indeed, one might be inclined to connect the formation of definite classes closely with the rise of a class of large mining-capitalists.

But this was a long process. Until 1870, at least, thousands of those who had once been ordinary workers had thousands of pounds in the bank at the end of the year thanks to gold- or copper-strikes.[113] By way of illustration, the eighty-six subscribers to the South Australian Mining Association (the Burra-Burra copper mine) were made up as follows[114]:

	with a capital of
18 small landowners	£3,850
11 tradesmen	£1,935
11 professional men	£765
10 gentlemen	£1,980
10 artisans	£115
8 farmers	£695
8 stock-holders	£1,865
5 auctioneers	£635
4 factory-owners	£510

and a great many of these had to scrape together their 'last shilling' in order to be able to buy a share, a share whose worth was increased sixfold within a very few weeks, and twelve-fold in a very few years, quite apart from annual dividends frequently of several hundred per cent.

A country which for almost a whole century revealed such astonishing social characteristics and tendencies naturally provided considerable opposition to any sociological classification embracing categories typical of European capitalist countries. This situation continued until towards the end of the nineteenth century, when, in a severe economic crisis, it turned away from all such sociological oddities and started to develop in an easily comprehensible way along with those categories associated with monopolistic capitalism.

But once a working class was formed, albeit slowly (a proletariat which was hereditary on only a very small scale), the conditions under which this process took place were completely different from those obtaining in the four countries previously investigated. The eight-hour day was the rule, modern machines were installed and these were worked principally by men, not primarily by women, and by children scarcely at all.

This was really a completely different type of working-class development from those of England, Germany, France or the United States of America.

India

We must now turn our attention to India, yet another fundamentally different country.

We must first consider the living conditions in Indian cities in the inter-war years. An official delegation of English trade unions reported:

We visited the workers' quarters wherever we stayed, and had we not seen them we could not have believed that such evil places existed. . . . Here is a group of houses in 'lines', the owner of which charges the tenant of each dwelling four shillings and sixpence a month as rent. Each house, consisting of one dark room used for all purposes, living, cooking and sleeping, is nine feet by nine feet, with mud walls and loose-tiled roof, and has a small open compound in front, a corner of which is used as the latrine. There is no ventilation in the living room except by a broken roof or that obtained through the entrance door when open. Outside the dwelling is a long narrow channel which receives the waste matter of all description and where flies and other insects abound. . . .

Outside all the houses on the edge of each side of the strip of land between the 'lines' are exposed gulleys, at some places stopped up with garbage, refuse and other waste matter, giving forth horrible smells repellent in the extreme. It is obvious that these gulleys are often used as conveniences especially by children. . . .

The overcrowding and insanitary conditions almost everywhere prevailing demonstrate the callousness and wanton neglect of their obvious duties by the authorities concerned.[115]

In fact, living conditions were sometimes so grim that in the hot season workers had to leave their hovels and move out of town merely to remain alive. They were forced to go into the country to beg or move into the already overcrowded peasant huts of their relatives. The report by the International Labour Office mentions times 'when workers are impelled to leave their improvised housing in some industrial centres during seasons of intense heat or epidemics of disease'.[116]

Even today a large portion of workers in India are only occasionally employed as industrial workers. For part of the year they go back to the land, where they form a section of what are called 'latent unemployed'.

In this connection the figures in Table 12, on absenteeism on the plantations in Mysore, are significant.[117] The reasons given for absence are: sickness, accidents, social and religious holidays, visits to their own villages where their families live, and so on.[118] One can imagine how difficult it is to maintain an industrial concern, and, more particularly, production, on an even keel. The main reason for this situation is to be found in the pitiful working conditions and general living standards of the

Table 12. Absenteeism on the plantations in Mysore[118], 1959.

	per cent		per cent		per cent
January	17·7	May	21·1	September	17·4
February	17·1	June	22·8	October	14·4
March	19·2	July	23·2	November	17·8
April	30·6	August	18·4	December	14·4

Table 13. Some industrial wages in India, 1955.

Wages in rupees (Rs 1 = 1s 6d)

	Oilers	Grinders	Ring-framepiecers
Bombay	9 0 0	5 12 0	4 2 0
Ahmedabad	7 5 6	11 0 0	6 15 0
Uttar Pradesh	2 0 0	3 0 0	3 0 0
Bengal	4 0 0	4 0 0	5 0 0
Madhiya Pradesh	8 2 0	8 2 0	1 10 0
Madras	4 0 0	9 0 0	4 0 0

employees. There can be no question here of a fully-employed working class; and we are not referring to interruptions of work through unemployment, as in Europe or the U.S.A.

Another aspect of the situation is this. In his book on the movement of industrial wages in India, published in 1955, R. Singh includes the wage-figures set out in Table 13.[119] In Bombay the oilers earn the highest wages, and the grinders almost two-fifths less. In Ahmedabad the grinder is the highest-paid and the oiler's wages are nearly two-fifths lower. In Uttar Pradesh grinders and piecers are paid at the same rate, in Bombay the oilers are paid twice as much as the piecers; but whereas in Bombay grinders and piecers earn roughly the same wages, it is oilers and piecers who do so in Madras.

It follows that in India at this time there could not be any question of a national labour-market on the lines of the Industrial Revolution in Europe; a market in which labour was sold at a national price.

This was at a time when, in all the works of the most modern exclusive concerns, throughout the country, carefully calculated, accurately and equally graded wage-scales had been introduced. Yet even in these concerns there were many workers to be found who returned from time to time to their 'family seat' to spend a short time there, badly fed but in a better atmosphere and away from the oppressive labour conditions of the city.

Russia under Tsarism, Australia during the first hundred years of its existence, India yesterday and today. How different and individual the circumstances were in which a working class was formed, and how fundamentally different they were not only from one another, but from the conditions in Europe and America at the time of the Industrial Revolution!

Historiography of the origins of the working class

In a study of the history of random sampling in official statistics. Kenessey remarks:

The first investigations into family living conditions were probably made in England, where capitalistic conditions of production created a new social class for whom the terms 'poor' and 'labouring' came to be used synonymously by contemporary scholars. This is openly stated in the title of Sir Frederick Morton Eden's book, published in London in 1797, *The state of the poor; or an history of the labouring classes in England from the Conquest to the present period with particular reference to their housing conditions, concerning food, clothing, heating and lodging, etc.* These early investigations were followed by others around 1790 both in England and on the Continent

Kenessey adds a footnote:

Nowadays people do not fully understand that, for the most part, it is not simply the investigations into family living-conditions which originate from the social problems of the nineteenth century, but also the European economic and social statistics, particularly in connection with the condition of the 'labouring class'. The setting-up of the well-known statistical societies in England around 1830 also took place in order to deal with these problems. As H. Westergaard says in a detailed article:

'There may be many reasons for the setting-up of these societies, but the most significant seems to have been an interest in social problems. . . . They wished to establish the whole truth about the condition of the poor classes of society.'

The Cornwall Polytechnic Society observed:

'Public attention was focused as intensively as never before on the physical and moral deterioration of the poorer classes in the capital and in many other cities.

The Glasgow Statistical Society saw their task as one of

'assembling facts, arranging and publishing them, to show up the condition and future prospects of humanity, with the aim of achieving improvements.'[1]

In addition to a mass of scientific and popular political literature there were numerous novels dealing with all ranks and classes of society. Marx observed in the *New York Daily Tribune* of 1 August 1854, in an article on 'The English Bourgeoisie':

The brilliant company of English novelists of our day, whose living, eloquent pages impart more political and social truths to the world than have been revealed in the words of all the professional politicians, political journalists and moralists put together, has described every stratum of the bourgeoisie, from the most aristocratic gentleman and investor in government stock who considers any sort of business to be 'common', to the small shopkeeper and barrister's clerk. And how have Dickens, Thackeray, Miss Bronte and Mrs Gaskell portrayed them? Full of arrogance, hypocrisy, petty tyranny and ignorance; and this condemnation was endorsed by the civilised world with the damning words with which it labelled this class: 'servile towards the high, tyrannical towards the low'.[2]

If this is what Marx says, we can add that there is, of course, no lack of employees, the working class, in these novels.

In addition the English government (the only one of any country to do so) added an inexhaustible series of parliamentary reports which brimmed over with information and permitted a profound, detailed insight into the conditions.

At about the same time, between 1830 and 1848, a flood of literature appeared in France, compiled by representatives of the bourgeoisie and petty bourgeoisie, and dealing with the wretched state of the workers, 'that disinherited branch of the family of mankind'.[3] 'Christian economists' like J. M. Gérando (*De la bienfaisance publique*), Morogues (*De la misère des ouvriers* and *Du paupérisme*), and A. de Villeneuve-Bargemont (*Économie politique chrétienne*), wrote about the poverty of employees. Pierre Leroux declared:

Before the Revolution of 1789 a worker earned in six days what a worker today earns in seven.[4]

Dupont-White described the condition of the workers:

They have no possessions, their lives become shorter and shorter, their food worse and worse, their whole stock and morality are rotting away.[5]

The 'Academy of moral and political sciences' awarded a prize to Buret's *Elend der arbeitenden Klassen in England und Frankreich* (1840), when Villermé, a doctor of medicine, had already embarked upon his investigations into the condition of French workers at the express desire of this same academy; investigations from which we have already quoted. In 1848, eight years after Villermé's and Buret's works were published, the elder Blanqui received a commission from the same academy to investigate the workers' condition (this investigation appeared in Paris in 1849 under the title of *Des classes ouvrières en France pendant l'année 1848*). All of them wanted reforms in order to forestall a revolution; all of them, whether 'non-political' humane philanthropists – De Précorbin preached *Philanthropie universelle*[6] – or died-in-the-wool conservatives like Villermé and the elder Blanqui, stood on the 'other side' of the barricades. What Naudet said of Villermé's work applied to them all[7]: 'A fight in the breach to defend society from the menace of socialism.'

There was a greater profusion of literature in Germany during the years before the 1848 revolution than in any other country. We owe this literary profusion[8] not principally to workers or members of the petty bourgeoisie, but to those representing the middle classes and lower aristocracy. There is only one explanation for this: the fact that the 'social question' in Germany was placed on the order-book by history under social conditions which were determined by the conflict between the middle classes and the aristocracy (this last was represented by the semi-feudal Junkers, the semi-feudal court, semi-feudal bureaucracy and the feudally-minded petty bourgeois), and not primarily by the antagonism between capital and labour.

Thus it was in these circumstances, and only in these circumstances, that the bourgeoisie was able to give evidence of the impoverishment of the industrial proletariat, in numerous publications, and likewise that the Junkers who controlled and subjugated industrial workers through the power of the state, were able to write about the impoverishment of industrial workers as a result of the growth of industrial capital. The middle class could, whether openly or by innuendo, lay the blame for the conditions on the ruling aristocracy, while the latter could shift the responsibility for the poverty and misery of the workers on to the capitalists who exploited them.

It was possible for this battle to be fought with a righteous fervour which was all the more intense because the bourgeoisie often suffered from a shortage of workmen through feudal restrictions, while the semi-feudal aristocracy dreaded the constant drain of labourers at the hands of the industrial middle classes. This means that those who were at the centre of the social question, including both the proletariat and those peasants about to join it, together with their children who were working as servants, were a matter of most intense interest to middle class and aristocracy alike, for entirely opposite reasons.

Such writings were supplemented by works of fiction dealing specifically with the weavers' condition. Among these were *Das Engelchen* by R. Prutz; and *Eisen, Gold und Geist* and *Weisse Sklaven oder die Leiden des Volkes* by Ernst Willkom.

Contemporary writings in the United States were less abundant than in Western and Central Europe, for conditions there were so vastly different; but it would be going too far to say there was a dearth of literature.

Not one of these works gave a really precise analysis of the rise of the working class. Many described their phenomenal emergence with amazement or horror, and some even advanced reasons, but none of them concentrated upon the actual process of their evolution. We can learn a good deal about our subject from contemporary writings, but this involves research. Some information is given in passing remarks which are often hidden in subordinate clauses or even in footnotes. Similarly there are important references in books on quite different topics, such as autobiographies, travel books, diaries, business correspondence.

The main theme of most socio-political documents is the condition of the workers, the misery of their lives, and possible ways of improving the circumstances of the proletariat, or even of doing away with the proletariat'. 'Doing away with the proletariat' means reducing it to penury; so to approach the problem in this way rules out any question of analysing a class.

No work of any significance devoted to the problems of the

Industrial Revolution appeared in England for a long time after these contemporary writings. Then Toynbee's *Lectures on the Industrial Revolution of the eighteenth century in England* was published: it was an historic work, in which the economic and social development of the Industrial Revolution was treated in a completely realistic manner, eminently readable even today. Until the appearance of *The Rise of Modern Industry* by the Hammonds in 1925, a number of important works were published based on Toynbee's concepts, especially in England, which showed no appreciable difference from ideas of prominent people at the time of the Industrial Revolution.

In 1926, with John Clapham's *An Economic History of Modern Britain*, the middle class evolved a new concept of the Industrial Revolution. The theory was advanced that past descriptions had viewed that epoch and the effect of the introduction of machinery on the proletariat far too 'pessimistically'; that there was no question of a radical worsening of the workers' condition during the Industrial Revolution; and that this was an assertion, unsubstantiated by the facts, made by Marxists and middle-class sentimentalists. Many English scholars, including T. S. Ashton and his followers in their recent works, have worked on the basis of this hypothesis. And although followers of Toynbee, the Webbs and the Hammonds have not died out, they are nevertheless in a minority in the western world today.

Marxist literature on the Industrial Revolution dates from Friedrich Engels' work *The Condition of the Working Classes in England*. True, this work describes the conditions during a somewhat later epoch, namely, the very end of the Industrial Revolution, but it abounds in important comments on the problems posed by that upheaval, applicable to any period of it. These observations by Engels and his later remarks in *Anti-Dühring*, together with the results of Marx's researches, and their analysis, which we find in *Capital*, laid the foundations of the Marxist conception of the Industrial Revolution.

During the following century no Marxist book appeared which

dealt specifically with the Industrial Revolution, and nothing written on this topic in other more comprehensive books took the opinions of Marx and Engels any further forward.

There was one important exception: V. I. Lenin's book on the development of capitalism in Russia. However, the fact that nearly half the book was concerned with questions of agriculture shows that Lenin did not devote either the main part of the work or specific sections of it to questions relating to the Industrial Revolution. Indeed, the words 'Industrial Revolution' do not appear in it.[9]

Only since the middle of the nineteen-fifties, when historians of socialist countries found more time to turn their attention towards their nations' earlier economic history, did the position begin to change. It is, of course, impossible to specify the exact date of these changes, as they were to a certain extent part of the social climate and received their first effective write-up almost accidentally in a speech, a pamphlet, or a chapter in a book. Only in this sense can we date the change in the middle class conception of the Industrial Revolution from Clapham's book, referred to above.

Similarly, one can date the start of the intensive study of this question of the Industrial Revolution in countires of the socialist camp from works which appeared in the early fifties by Gyula, Lederer and V. Sandor (Hungary), Klima and Purš (Czecho-slovakia), W. Kula (Poland) and finally from a speech by Kuczyn-ski at the beginning of May 1956 in the History Institute of the Polish Academy of Sciences in Warsaw, on the Industrial Revolution in England and Germany.[10] What is new in Kuczynski's speech and resulting interpretation of the Industrial Revolution is the sharp distinction between the 'classical form' in England and the special features of the Central and Eastern European form, which are associated with Lenin's so-called Prussian form of agricultural development.[11]

Toynbee's important work began a more serious analysis of the structure of the classes of people in employment. The latest major work to deal with this problem appeared in 1963 under the specific title *The Making of the English Working Class* by E. P. Thompson.[12]

Scarcely any other subject in human social history has produced a literature in which such a mass of valuable essays has appeared from all classes and ranks of society, not to mention unsuccessful works. Thus Marxists still quote a vast number of middle-class writings, with good reason, as they did one hundred years ago; and conversely, members of the middle classes quote Marxists. Yet there is a curious kind of class relationship to be observed in this literature. True, there are numerous social analyses, more or less successful, in which the author has been intellectually gripped by the theme of his research, regardless of his own 'private' point of view. But there is no work on the rise and condition of the working class which has not suffered intellectual shipwreck if the author has not been sympathetic towards this class. In Dante's Inferno there are regions inhabited by the most pitiful human vermin suffering the most terrible torments; and how marvellously he depicts them. No one, however, who did not at least feel sympathetic towards the poor, or a deep religious responsibility for their situation has ever been able to present an analysis of the working class or a description of their condition of any intellectual merit.

Notes and bibliography

Introduction

1. W. J. Ashley, *An English Economic History and Theory*, London, 1893, Part II, p 255ff.
2. National Archives, Potsdam, Pr. Br. Rep. 30A, Tit 3, No. 3a.
3. F. L. Olmstead, *Journey in the Seaboard Slave States*, New York, 1859, p 47.

1 Workers before the Industrial Revolution

1. An analysis of these accounts is given by J. Kuczynski, *Die Geschichte der Lage der Arbeiter unter dem Kapitalismus*, Berlin, 1964, Vol 22, p 33ff. This book describes the conditions of the workers in England from 1640 to 1760.
2. Cf. Christopher Hill, *The century of revolution*, Edinburgh, 1961, p 131, and in particular, *Lieutenant-Colonel John Lilburne's Apologetical Narrative relating to his illegal and unjust sentence*, Amsterdam, April 1652.
3. Anatole France, *Les dieux ont soif*, Oeuvres complètes, tome XX, Paris, 1931, p 169ff.
4. Friedrich Engels, *Die Lage der arbeitenden Klasse in England*, Berlin, 1952, p 31ff.
5. G. Heitz, *Ländliche Leinenproduktion in Sachsen 1470–1555*, Berlin, 1961, p 59
6. G. Martin, *La Grande Industrie* à *l'époque de Louis XIV*, Paris, 1899, p 115ff.
7. Published by Julien Hayem: *Mémoires et documents*, First Series, p 115ff.
8. Henri Sée, *Histoire économique de la France. Le Moyen Age et l'Ancien Régime*, Paris, 1939, p 266ff.
9. M. Bouvier-Ajam and Gilbert Mury, *Les classes sociales en France*, Paris, 1963, Vol I, p 286.
10. Central German archives, Merseburg, Rep. 9 C 6c 1, 15 Dec. 1687.
11. H. W. Wagnitz, *Historische Nachrichten und Bemerkungen über die merkwürdigsten Zuchthäuser in Deutschland*. 2 vols (Halle a.d. Saale 1791–4) II, 2, p 22.
12. ibid. I, p 347.
13. H. Krüger, *Zur Geschichte der Manufakturen und der Manufacturarbeiter in Preussen*, Berlin, 1958, p 142

14 National archives, Dresden, document on deputation for national economy, manufacture and commerce, Loc. 5356, Vol I, sheet 122.

15 ibid.

16 R. Forberger, *Die Manufaktur in Sachsen vom Ende des 16. bis zum Anfang des 19. Jahrhunderts*, Berlin, 1958, p 68.

17 J. E. Neale, *Elizabeth I and her parliaments*, Vol II, London, 1957, p 338.

18 R. Page Arnot, *A history of the Scottish miners from the earliest times*, London, 1955, p 7.

19 G. D. H. Cole, *Studies in class structure*, London, 1955, p 31.

20 Vincent van Gogh in his letters to his brother Theo: *Als Mensch unter Menschen*, Berlin, 1963, Vol I, p 101ff.

21 J. Möser, *Patriotische Phantasien*, Berlin, 1868, Part I, p. 341.

22 G. Schmoller, *Umrisse und Untersuchungen zur Verfassungs-, Verwaltungs- und Wirtschaftsgeschichte*, Leipzig, 1898, p 455.

23 G. Schmoller, *Zur Geschichte der deutschen Kleingewerbe im 19. Jahrhundert*, Halle, 1870, p 14.

24 c.f. R. B. Morris, *Government and labor in early America*, New York, 1946, p 38.

25 Jean Fourastin, *Machinisme et bien-être*, Paris, 1962, p 48.

26 S. le Prêtre de Vauban, *Dixme royale* ed Coornaert, p. 274ff.

27 *Die soziale Frage in der deutschen Geschichte mit besonderer Berücksichtigung des ehemaligen Fürstentums Waldeck-Pyrmont*, Wiesbaden, 1964, p 3ff.

28 W. Conze, Vom 'Pöbel' zum 'Proletariat', *Vierteljahresschrift für Sozial- und Wirtschaftsgeschichte*, Vol 41, Wiesbaden, 1954, Book 4, p 335ff.

29 The question here is: who were subordinate to or outside the social order? Clearly they were 'trades' or rather people who were not of use to society and were indifferent to society or a danger to it: vagrants, gypsies, harlots, a night-wandering rabble, leading a hand-to-mouth existence, making money more often than not by robbing and cheating. 'The gathering of gypsies and other louts caused considerable inconvenience; few such people were endurable and their large numbers became a great nuisance to the whole countryside, as they caused severe loss and damage to the already impoverished villeins by their robbery and pilfering. The louts did not indulge in begging or petty larcency, but went in for serious crime, which terrified the population.'

The seventeenth and eighteenth centuries are here dealt with in a worthy study by Hermann Arnold, *Vaganten, Komödianten, Fieranten und Briganten*, Stuttgart, 1958, p 4.

30   G. Ortes, *Della economia nazionale*, lib. 6, Scrittori classici italiani di economia politica, parte moderna, T 21, Milan, 1804.

2 The working class emerges

1   Central German archives, Merseburg, Rep 74, K 3 VIII, No 24, sheet 90ff.
2   K. Marx, *Das Kapital*, Vol I, Berlin, 1962, p 674.
3   ibid. p 465.
4   ibid. p 455.
5   K. Biedermann, *Vorlesungen über Socialismus und sociale Fragen*, Leipzig, 1847, p 55ff.
6   C. Babbage, *On the economy of machinery and manufactures*, London, 1833.
7   Von Arnim, under the pseudonym Suederus, op. cit., p. 39.
8   F. Engels, *Herrn Eugen Dührings Umwälzung der Wissenschaft*, Berlin, 1948, p 321.
9   F. Schleiermacher, *Mologen. Eine Neujahrsgabe*, Berlin, 1800, p 71ff.
10   D. Nisard, *Mélanges*, Paris, 1838, p 370.
11   Engels, op. cit., p 31.
12   cf. J. Kuczynski, *Darstellung der Lage der Arbeiter in England von 1760 bis 1832*, Berlin, 1964, Vol 23, p 5.
13   cf. among recently published works especially N. J. Smelser, *Social change in the Industrial Revolution*, London, 1959.
14   F. Engels, *Die Lage*, (op. cit.), p 37.
15   cf. R. Forberger, op. cit., p 138ff; J. Kuczynski, op. cit., Vol I, Berlin, 1961, p 27ff; K. Marx, Vol I, op. cit., p 450ff.
16   E. P. Thompson, *The making of the English working class*, London, 1963, p 587ff.
17   Speech on 27 February 1812 by George Gordon, Lord Byron.
18   Aspinall, *Early English Trade Unions*, p 116. Quoted in Morton and Tate *The British Labour Movement 1770–1920*, London, 1956, p 36.
19   H. Sée, *Französische Wirtschaftsgeschichte*, Vol. II, Jena, 1936, p 191.
20   National archives, Dresden, district prefecture Zwickau, No 260, motion concerning the complaint lodged with His Majesty by the

236

merchant Johann Friedrich Haussner jun. at Plauen by reason of the prohibition of the local council against setting up a mechanical cotton-spinning works within the said town.

21 Central German archives, Merseburg, Rep 120 B II 1, No 5, Vol I.

22 L. R. Villermé, *Tableau de l'état physique et moral des ouvriers employés dans les manufactures de coton, de laine et de soie*, Vol I, Paris, 1840, p 26.

23 V. Hugo: 'Ces enfants dont pas un seul ne rit' *Mélancholie*.

24 J. R. Commons et al. (edd), *A documentary history of American industrial society*, Vol VI, Cleveland, 1910, p 217.

25 F. Engels, *Die Lage* (op. cit.) p 204ff.

26 Report by Committee on Education relative to the education of children employed in manufacturing establishments. House of Representatives, Commonwealth of Massachusetts, 17 March 1836.

27 E. Abbott, *Women in industry*, New York, 1910, p 58ff.

28 cf. H. R. Warfel, *Noah Webster, schoolmaster to America*, New York, 1936, p 209.

29 *Report on the Production and Manufacture of Cotton*, 1832, p 16. The Convention of the Friends of Domestic Industry, which organised this investigation, assumed that all the handloom-weavers in the factories were men, so that the percentage of 58.1 for women is probably too low.

30 *Boston Courier*, 27 June 1833. For the same period (1832) the employment of women in the entire cotton industry of Massachusetts is put at 158 per cent of that of men. See *Trends in the American economy in the nineteenth century. Studies of income and wealth*, Vol XXIV, Princeton, 1960, p 460.

31 J. R. Commons et al. (edd.), op. cit., Vol V, p 64.

32 ibid., p 62

33 P. S. Foner, *History of the labor movement in the United States*, New York, 1947, p 65.

34 Papers published by the Board of Trade, Vol IV, p 382ff.; quoted from J. R. McCulloch, *A statistical account of the British Empire*, London, 1837, Vol II, p 80.

35 K. A. Gerlach, *Die Bedeutung des Arbeiterinnenschutzes*, Jena, 1913,

36 cf. also C. Wilson, 'The entrepreneur in the Industrial Revolution in Britain', in *History*, London, 1957, Vol XLII, p 115.

37 Speech by Deputy Degenkolb in a debate in the Prussian Chamber on 9 and 10 May 1863, when a government plan was put forward to limit child-labour. Quoted in G. K. Anton, *Geschichte der preussischen*

Fabrikgesetzgebung bis zu ihrer Aufnahme durch die Reichsgewerbe-ordnung, Berlin, 1953, (new ed.) p 158.

38 T. Carlyle, *Chartism*, London, 1870, p 21.

39 K. Marx, op. cit., p 416.

40 Hobsbawm, *The Age of Revolution*, London and New York 1964, p 70.

41 Central German archives, Merseburg, Rep 74, K 3 VIII, No 24, sheet 87ff.

42 E. Michel, (translated from German translation) *Sozialgeschichte der industriellen Arbeiterwelt*, Frankfurt-am-Main, 1960, p 79.

43 Factory Inspectors' Reports, London, December 1838, App. V, p 98.

44 G. Nicholls, *History of the English poor law*, London 1854, Vol II, pp 18 & 58.

45 A. Redford, *The economic history of England, 1760–1860*, London, 1931, pp 44ff, 56ff.

46 H. Sée, op. cit., Vol II, p 237.

47 Fourteenth Annual Report, Bureau of Statistics of Labor, Massachusetts, Boston, 1883, p 380.

48 Quoted in the address to the working men of Massachusetts, 1834, from J. R. Commons et al. (edd.) op. cit., Vol I, p 429.

49 Anon., *Über den vierten Stand und die socialen Reformen*, Magdeburg, 1844, p 12.

50 H. Bettziech (alias BETA), *Geld und Geist. Versuch einer Sichtung und Erlösung der arbeitenden Volks-Kraft*, Berlin, 1845, p 8ff.

51 E. Michel, op. cit., p 80ff.

52 Hobsbawm, op. cit., p 70.

53 G. Weerth, *Fragment eines Romans*, Complete Works, Berlin, 1956, Vol II, p 226ff.

54 *Journal des débats*, Paris, 9 September 1831, quoted by Hobsbawm, op. cit., p 238.

55 W. Cooke Taylor, *Notes of a tour in the manufacturing districts of Lancashire in a series of letters to His Grace the Archbishop of Dublin*, London, 1842, p 6ff.

8 The working class: its habits of thought and action

1 F. Engels, op. cit., p 7

2 H. W. Bensen, *Die Proletarier. Eine historische Denkschrift*, Stuttgart, 1847, p 17ff.

238

3 District archives, Meiningen, Inneres alt, 24, 10, Police office, sheet 10ff

4 *Allgemeine Preussische Zeitung*, 31 October, 1 & 7 November 1845.

5 T. Mundt, *Die Geschichte der Gesellschaft in ihren neueren Entwicklunger und Problemen*, Berlin, 1844, p 188ff.

6 E. Hobsbawm, op. cit., p 248ff.

7 V. Hugo, *Les Châtiments*, Brussels, 1853.

8 A. Blanqui, *Les classes ouvrières en France pendant l'année 1848* Paris, 1849, p 98ff.

9 Cf. Robert Owen, *Observations on the effects of the manufacturing system*, 2nd ed., London, 1817, p 16. 'Since the general introduction o expensive machinery, human nature has been forced far beyond it average strength.'

10 K. Marx, op. cit., Vol I, p 425ff.

11 J. R. Commons, op. cit., Vol I, p 159ff.

12 This table is compiled from the following sources:—

    Prussia: Reinick, 'Effects of the duty on flour and slaughtered mea in the period 1838–1861', *Zeitschrift des Königlich Preussischen Statistischen Bureaus*, Jg. 3, Berlin, September 1863. and A. Spiethoff, *Die wirtschaftlichen Wechsellagen*, Vol II Tübingen and Zürich, 1955.

    Leipzig: O. Gerlach, 'Meat-consumption in Leipzig', *Jahrbücher für Nationalökonomie und Statistik*, N.F., Vol II, Jena, 1889.

    Munich: G. Mayr, 'Die Fleischnahrung der Münchener Bevölkerung'. *Zeitschrift des Königlich Bayerischen Statistischen Bureaus* Jg. 3, Munich, 1871, and G. Gschwendtner, *Die Entwicklung der Münchener Fleischpreise seit Beginn des 19, Jahrhundert: und ihre Ursachen*, Diessen, 1911.

    Lübeck: G. H. Schmidt, *Statistik des Consums in Lübeck von 1836–68* Jena, 1891.

    Hamburg: *Beiträge zur Statistik Hamburgs, mit besonderer Berücksichtigung auf die Jahre 1821–1852*, Hamburg, 1854.

13 F. de Tapiès, *La France et l'Angleterre ou statistique morale et physique de la France comparée à celle de l'Angleterre sur tous les points analogues* Paris, 1845, p 54.

14 M. A. Legoyt, *La France statistique*, Paris, 1843, second appendix t the table of French consumption.

15 cf. E. J. Hobsbawm, *Labouring men. Studies in the history of labour* London, 1964, p 84.

16 R. M. Hartwell, 'The rising standard of living in England, 1800–1850', *The Economic History Review*, Second Series, Vol XIII, Utrecht 1961, No 3, April.

17 R. O. Cummings, *The American and his food. A history of food habits in the United States*, Chicago, 1941, pp 55 & 90.

18 H. Mayhew, *London Labour and the London Poor*, London, 1861, Vol II, p 192.

19 M. Gorki, *Mother*, Moscow, 1950, p 7, tr. Margaret Wettlin.

20 K. Marx, F. Engels, *Werke*, Berlin, 1956, Vol I, p 417.

21 The consumption of spirits during the first forty years of the eighteenth century are reported to have increased six times!

22 J. Kuczynski, *Die Geschichte der Lage der Arbeiter*, Vol XXII, p 242.

23 M. Mohl, *Uber die württembergische Gewerbsindustrie*, Stuttgart and Tübingen, 1828, p 52.

24 National archives, Saxony, Ministry of National Education, No 3353, documents on factory school matters, sheet 132.

25 *Journal of the Statistical Society of London*, London, 1839, Vol II, pp 74 and 83.

26 cf. also F. A. Artz, *France under the Bourbon Restoration*, Cambridge, Mass., 1931, p 139.

27 Hansard, IX, p 798 mn, quoted by J. L. and B. Hammond, *The town labourer*, London, 1937, p 70.

28 L. T. Hobhouse and J. L. Hammond, *Lord Hobhouse, a memoir*, London, 1905, p 30ff.

29 M. Gorki, op. cit., pp. 6 & 7.

30 F. Engels, *Anti-Dühring*, p 222.

31 ibid., p 222ff.

32 Macaulay's speech on the ten-hour day in Macaulay, *Prose and Poetry*, London, 1952, pp 771–4.

33 Quoted from *A documentary history of American industrial society*, Vol IX, p 279.

34 'A reduction of hours, an increase of wages', quoted ibid., p 284.

35 ibid., p 289ff.

36 H. Sée, *Les origines du capitalisme moderne*, Paris, 1926, p 190.

37 A. Hutt, *British trade unionism*, 5th ed., London, 1962, p 8.

38 S. and B. Webb, *The history of trade unionism*, revised edition extended to 1920, London, 1926, p 87.

39 F. Engels, *Die Lage*, (op. cit.), p 206.

40 Quoted from *Fourteenth annual report of the Bureau of Statistics of Labor*, Massachusetts, Boston, 1883, p 391.

41 S. Simpson, *The working man's manual*, Philadelphia, 1831, p 86.

42 cf. also R. Strauss, *Die Lage und die Bewegung der Chemnitzer Arbeiter in der ersten Hälfte des 19. Jahrhunderts*, Berlin, 1960, p 171ff.

43 E. Hobsbawm, *The Age of Revolution*, London, New York, 1964, p 254ff.

44 Max Morris (ed.), *From Cobbett to the Chartists 1815–1848*, London, 1954, p 153.

45 Originally appeared as foreword to K. Marx, *Enthüllungen über den Kommunistenprozess zu Köln*, 3rd ed., 1855.

46 J. Watson, *A memoir*, 1879, p 14ff., quoted in Max Morris (ed.), op. cit.

47 I. F. C. Harrison, *Learning and Living 1790–1960*, London, 1961, p 59.

48 A. Smith, *An introductory lecture on the past and present state of science in this country, as regards the working classes, delivered at the Ripon Mechanics' Institute, on Friday 29 April 1831*, Ripon, 1831, p 19, quoted in I. F. C. Harrison, op. cit.

49 *The working man's friend and family instructor*, Vol I, London, January–March 1850.

50 *Life and letters of Frederick W. Robertson*, London, 1891, Vol I, p 54.

4 The rise of the working class: national differences

1 F. Engels, e.g. in *Die Lage* (op. cit.), p. 42.

2 A. Toynbee, *Lectures on the Industrial Revolution of the eighteenth century in England*, London, 1884.

3 P. Mantoux, *The Industrial Revolution in the eighteenth century*, London, 1929.

4 J. L. and B. Hammond, *The skilled labourer, 1760–1832*, and *The village labourer, 1760–1832*, London, 1911.

5 C. R. Fay, *Great Britain from Adam Smith to the present day*, London, 1928.

6 Recently, E. Hobsbawm, p 44, has given 1780 as an approximate date, thus following T. S. Ashton (T. S. Ashton, *An economic history of England: the eighteenth century*, London, 1955, p 125.) H. Mottek (H. Mottek, H. Blumberg, H. Wutzmer and W. Becker, *Studien zur Geschichte der Industriellen Revolution in Deutschland*, Berlin, 1960, p. 12ff.) follows a similar line. Yet even if the number of scholars who

are inclined to place the beginning of the Industrial Revolution somewhat later has in fact grown during the last twenty years, I do not consider their arguments valid. Cf. my *Geschichte der Lage der Arbeiter*, Vol XXIII, p 10ff.

7 *Cambridge Economic History*, London, 1965, Vol VI, p 274ff.
8 Cf. A. P. Wadsworth and J. de Lacy Mann, *The cotton trade and industrial Lancashire, 1600–1780*, Manchester, 1931, p 425, and J. T. Ward, *The factory movement 1830–1855*, London, 1962, p 8.
9 Notwithstanding that, single wool factories were set up. A worsted factory near Lancaster began, in 1784, with mechanical spinning.
10 '*A Modest Proposal for preventing the Children of Poor People from being a burthen to their Parents, or the Country, and for making them Beneficial to the Publick*.
11 Archibald Alison, High Sheriff of Lanarkshire, *The principles of Population, and their connection with Human Happiness*, 2 vols, 1840. The Alison referred to is the historian of the French Revolution and, like his brother, Dr W. P. Alison, a diehard Tory.
12 F. Engels, *Die Lage* (op. cit.), p 130.
13 Milesian: an old Irish family.
14 T. Carlyle, *Chartism*, London, 1840, pp 28 & 31ff.
15 F. Engels, op. cit., p 131ff.
16 J. C. Drummond and A. Wilbraham, *The Englishman's food. A history of five centuries of English diet*, London, 1939, p 205.
17 L. Braddon, *The miseries of the poor*, London, 1722, p 18.
18 In the sixteenth and seventeenth centuries the word 'yeoman' denoted tenant farmers and peasant proprietors; Arthur Young used it only in the sense of peasant proprietors, and the nineteenth-century writers used it in this narrower sense. But many authors of the eighteenth century, including Adam Smith, used it in its older and wider meaning.
19 G. M. Trevelyan, *History of England*, London, 1926, pp 524–5.
20 W. Cobbett, *Political Register*, 15 March 1806, London.
21 L. Brentano, *Eine Geschichte der wirtschaftlichen Entwicklung Englands*, Jena, 1929, Vol III, p 8.
22 G. D. H. Cole, *Studies in class structure*, London, 1955, p 31.
23 W. Bowden, *Industrial society in England towards the end of the eighteenth century*, New York, 1925, p 99.
24 F. Le Play, *Les ouvriers européens. Tome troisième, Les ouvriers du Nord*, Tours, 1877, p 315.

242

25 Figures for European towns are given by Gustav Sundbarg, *Aperçus statistiques internationaux*, 11th year, Stockholm 1908. Since that time the figures have been constantly revised for individual towns, but without producing any more comparable dates from which conclusions may be drawn.

26 F. Engels, op. cit., p 375.

27 M. R. Benedict, *Farm policies of the United States 1790–1950*, New York, 1953, p 18.

28 Cf. *A discourse delivered at Schenectady, July 26th 1826 before the New York Alpha of the Phi Beta Kappa*, Ballston Spa, N.Y. 1826.

29 D. W. Mitchell, *Ten years in the United States*, London, 1862, p 193.

30 Cf. e.g. Evans' circular *Vote yourself a farm*.

31 C. Goodrich and S. Davison, 'The wage earner in the westward movement', *Political Science Quarterly*, No 50, 1935, No 51, 1936, No 53, 1937. Cf. also Fred Shannon, 'The Homestead Act and the labor surplus', *American Historical Review*, No 61, 1936, and 'post mortem on the labor-safety-valve theory', *Agricultural History*, No 19, Illinois, 1945.

32 W. J. Bromwell, *History of immigration to the United States*, New York, 1856.

33 S. Luther, *Address to the working-men of New England*, Boston, 1832.

34 C. A. Murray, *Travels in North America*, London, 1839, Vol II, p 298.

35 Cf also H. Commager (ed.), *Immigration and American history*, Minneapolis, 1961, p 55ff.

36 G. Myers, *History of the great American fortunes*, Chicago, 1911, Vol I, p 93ff.

37 Quoted in R. Ernst, 'The economic status of the New York City negroes 1850–1863', *Negro History Bulletin*, XII, March, 1949. Even as late as 1900 there was a song with the refrain: 'No Irish need apply.'

38 Cf. also L. F. Litwack, *North of slavery*, Chicago, 1961, p 162ff.

39 Cf. also J. H. Franklin, *From slavery to freedom*, New York, 1947.

40 Cf. also R. B. Morris, *Government and labor in early America*, New York, 1947, p 182ff.

41 H. Wish, *Society and thought in early America*, New York, 1950, p. 487.

42 H. Clews, *Twenty-eight years in Wall Street*, New York, 1888, p 75.

43 R. B. Morris, op. cit., p 47.

44 C. Bridenbaugh, *Cities in the wilderness*, New York, 1955, p 359.

45 There were also 'ordinary' bond-slaves who should be ranked with them.

46 We make this assertion as there were Indian slaves too. In isolated areas, in the early days, they were often in considerable numbers. Thus it is reported that in South Carolina, in 1708, there were four thousand one hundred Negro and one thousand four hundred Indian slaves.

47 E. B. Greene (*The revolutionary generation*, New York, 1943, p 68ff.) calculates the number of people who were not free to be one third – as I do.

48 R. B. Morris, op. cit., p 36.

49 Cf. *Historical statistics of the United States, colonial times to 1957*, Washington D.C., 1960, p 9.

50 *Historical statistics of the United States 1789–1945*, Washington D.C., 1949, p 27.

51 R. G. Layer, *Earnings of cotton mill operatives, 1825–1914*, Cambridge, 1955, p 70ff.

52 G. S. Gibb, *The Saco-Lowell shops*, Cambridge, 1950, p 53.

53 Cf. the letter entitled *A documentary history of American industrial society*, Vol VIII, p 169.

54 'The poor and the poor laws of Great Britain', *The Biblical Repertory and Princeton Review*, XIII, January 1841.

55 A. Brisbane, *Social destiny of man*, Philadelphia, 1840.

56 E. Kellog, *Labor and other capital*, New York, 1849.

57 *American and British Technology in the 19th Century*, London, 1962, p 4.

58 M. Chevalier, *Society, manners and politics in the United States*, Boston, 1839, p 143ff.

59 V. M. Dalin, *Babeuf-Studien*, Berlin, 1961, p 7.

60 F. Engels, *Anti-Dühring*, p 324.

61 ibid., p 317ff.

62 E. Hobsbawm, *The Age of Revolution*, p 145ff.

63 The years between 1815 and 1848 saw the French press at its highest peak of development. The historians Mignet, Thiers and Thierry were either journalists or wrote regularly and prolifically for the press. Great literary criticism appeared in the press: one has only to think of Sainte-Beuve's essays. Famous novels of the age were first published as serials, as those of Alexandre Dumas and Eugène Sue; the best

known caricaturists of that epoch influenced the press, with Daumier at their head. Balzac wrote a memorandum on the press. The latter seems to have been important enough at the time for an English historian of today to be guilty of the grotesque statement: 'Louis-Philippe became King of the French as a result of a revolution begun by the newspapers.' (J. Collins, *The government and the newspaper press in France 1814–1881*, London, 1959, p 60.

64 A detailed account of the strikes of these years is given in J. P. Aguet, *Les grèves sous la Monarchie de Juillet – 1830–1847*, Geneva, 1954. Isolated strikes and rebellions in the early years are dealt with also in Paul Gonnet, *Esquisse de la crise économique et sociale*, Paris, 1955.

65 P. J. Proudhon, *Manuel du spéculateur à la Bourse*, Paris, 1857.

66 Lysis (E. Le Tailleur), *Contre l'oligarchie financière*, Paris, 1908.

67 P. Combe, *Niveau de vie et progrès technique en France (1860–1939)*, Paris, 1956.

68 R. E. Cameron, *France and the economic development of Europe 1800–1914*, Princeton, 1961 and 'Economic growth and stagnation in France, 1815–1914', *The Journal of Modern History*, Chicago, March 1958, Vol XXX, No 1.

69 D. S. Landes, 'French entrepreneurship and industrial growth in the nineteenth century', *Journal of Economic History*, 1949, Vol IX.

70 F. Engels, *Die Bauernfrage in Frankreich und Deutschland*, Berlin 1951, p 3.

71 J. Laffitte, *Réflexions sur la réduction de la rente et sur l'état du crédit* Paris, 1824.

72 K. Marx, F. Engels, *Kleine ökonomische Schriften*, Berlin 1955, p 319

73 Cf. also C. H. Pouthas, *La population française pendant la première moitié du XIXe siècle*, Paris, 1956, p 193.

74 H. Sée, op. cit., Vol II, p 128

75 Ibid., p 179.

76 Cf. enquiries made about the Comité du Travail of 1848 by Agricol Perdiguier, *Mémoires d'un compagnon*, Moulins, 1914, ('Cahiers du Centre'); and E. Levasseur, *Histoire des classes ouvrières*, Vol II p 211ff.

77 H. Sée, op. cit., Vol II, p 244ff.

78 P. Louis, *Histoire du mouvement syndical en France (1789–1910)* Paris, 1911, p 93.

79 J. Alazard, 'Les causes de l'insurrection lyonnaise de novembre 1831'

Revue historique, 1912; Lévy-Schneider, 'Le gouvernement insurrectionnel de l'Hôtel de ville et L. M. Pierenon', *Revue d'histoire de Lyon*, 1910, p 161ff., p 241ff.; E. Tarle, *Der Lyoner Arbeiteraufstand.* Marx-Engels-archiv, Frankfurt, 1927, Vol II. Tarle has rightly emphasised the great repercussions of the November rebellion of 1831. He gives notable extracts from an article in the *Journal des Débats*, in which it was stated with some horror that a real class struggle was brewing; and from declarations in the *Globe* written by Saint-Simon's disciples. They set themselves up as apostles hovering over the battlefield. Cf. also F. Dutacq, 'Les journées lyonnaises de novembre 1831', *La Révolution française*, June–August 1932, and Justin Godart, 'Les événements de novembre 1831 à Lyon', *Révolution de 1848*, No 143, December 1932.

80 H. Sée, op. cit., p 259.
81 J. W. Goethe, *Jübiläumsausgabe* by Cotta, Stuttgart and Berlin, Vol IV, p 228.
82 K. Immermann, *Die Epigonen*, Düsseldorf, 1836, Vol I, p 8ff.
83 Ibid., p 280.
84 Ibid., p 334.
85 Ibid., Vol III, p 35ff.
86 K. Immermann, *Münchhausen*, Berlin, 1955, p 17.
87 C. O. Müller, *Briefe aus einem Gelehrtenleben 1797–1840*, Berlin, 1950, p 1ff.
88 L. Geiger, *Therese Huber 1764 bis 1829. Leben und Briefe einer deutschen Frau*, Stuttgart, 1901, p 235.
89 *Briefe von Alexander v. Humboldt an Varnhagen v. Ense aus den Jahren 1827 bis 1858*, Leipzig, 1860, p 90.
90 Cf. ibid. p 118 and K. Hegel, *Leben und Erinnerungen*, Leipzig, 1900, p 38.
91 Husband of Helena Christiane, daughter of Johan Caspar Harkort III (1716–61).
92 E. Soeding, *Die Harkorts*, Münster, 1957, p 638.
93 H. Simon, *Ein Gedenkbuch für das deutsche Volk*, Berlin, 1865, Part I, p 140ff.
94 *Hundert Jahre Mech. Baumwoll-Spinnerei und Weberei Augsburg* (place and year of publication unknown) p 68ff.
95 Central German archives, Merseburg, Rep. 89 H, Abt. XIII, No 1, Vol II, decrees by the royal civil cabinet, 1st part; concerning the

246

conditions and state of tradespeople – measures to help them and to employ out-of-work factory-workers, sheet 34 v.

96 K. Lärmer, *Geschichte der Arbeitsordnungen im Mansfelder Kupfer-schieferbergbau vom feudalen 18. Jahrhundert bis zum Jahre 1945*, Dissertation, Berlin, 1958, p 147ff.
97 National archives, Magdeburg, Rep. F 8, 18, Vol I, sheet 58.
98 Ibid.
99 Central German archives, Merseburg, Rep 121, Abt. B, Tit. IX, Sekt. 6, No 1, sheet 13.
100 Ibid., No 109.
101 Ibid., No. 1.
102 National archives Magdeburg, Rep. F8, XXIII, 19, Vol III, sheets 85–88.
103 Ibid.
104 K. Lärmer, op. cit., p 152ff.
105 H. Paul, *Zur Frage der Übereinstimmung der Produktionsverhältnisse mit dem Charakter der Produktivkräfte beim Übergang vom Feudalismus zum Kapitalismus in der Landwirtschaft Preussens*, Dissertation, Leipzig 1957, p 263.
106 D. Eichholtz, *Junker und Bourgeoisie vor 1848 in der preussischen Eisenbahngeschichte*, Berlin, 1962, p 184.
107 Year 1844, No 97, 4 December.
108 K. V. Basilevitsch, S. V. Bachruschin, A. M. Pankratova, A. V. Focht, *History of the U.S.S.R.*, Moscow, 1950, Part III, p 8ff.
109 The contradictory statement by S. B. Liljegren (*Aspects of Australia in contemporary literature*, Upsala and Copenhagen, 1962, p 17) has not been proved by him.
110 Cf. e.g. letter of the Governor L. MacQuarie to J. T. Bigge in 1819, which in recent literature has been printed by R. Ward, *The Australian Legend*, Melbourne, 1958, p 30. Ward also produces contemporary literature on this topic.
111 G. C. Mundy, *Our Antipodes; or residence and rambles in the Australian colonies with a glimpse of the gold fields*, 3rd ed., London, 1855. On the subject of the movement between rich and poor, the author wrote:
'In England there are isolated cases – especially in industry – in which one man or another, in the course of a long life, has raised himself and his family from modest circumstances to a position of enormous wealth; but in Australia certain men have run the whole gamut of grades between adventurous begging and an unusually

extensive property within one quarter of the normal human span.'
J. Hood (*Australia and the East*, London, 1843) described how many
of the finest houses in Sydney were owned by people of very poor
origins. A small manor-house went by the name of Frying-pan Hall,
since its owner had been a smith after serving a seven-year sentence.
This movement between classes naturally took place in all territories
predominantly colonised by whites. But in Australia this movement,
though it existed, did so without there being (in contrast to the United
States) a landed aristocracy with permanent slaves, or a settled
financial or industrial middle class. (Translation from the German
translation.)

12 W. E. Murphy, *The history of capital and labour in all lands and ages*,
    Sydney, 1888, p 132.

13 Cf. detailed accounts, e.g. in D. Pike, *Paradise of dissent. South
    Australia 1829–1857*, London, 1957, Ch. XVIII.

14 South Australian Archives, quoted in D. Pike, op. cit., p 332.

15 A. A. Purcell and J. Hallworth, *Report on labour conditions in India.*
    Trades Union Congress, London, 1928, p 8ff.

16 *Industrial labour in India*. International Labour Office. Studies and
    Reports, Ser. A (Industrial Relations), No 41 (Geneva) p 159. For
    the living conditions of industrial workers, cf. also S.C. Aggarwal,
    Industrial housing in India, New Delhi, 1952; cf. also K. N. Srivastava,
    Industrial peace and labour in India, Allahabad, 1955, Ch. VII.

17 *The Indian Labour Year Book 1959*, New Delhi, 1960.

18 B. R. Misra, (*Report on socio-economic survey of Jamshedpur city*,
    Patna, 1959) informs us (p 127) that his researches in 1954–5 showed
    that forty-four per cent of absenteeism was due to sickness.

19 R. Singh, *Movement of industrial wages in India*, Bombay and Calcutta,
    1955, p 73.

Historiography of the origins of the working class

1 Z. Kenessey, *Zur geschichtlichen Entwicklung des Stichprobenverfahrens
   in der amtlichen Statistik* in *Allgemeines statistisches Archiv*, 48th year,
   Wiesbaden, 1964, p 315.

2 K. Marx, F. Engels, *Werke*, Berlin, 1961, Vol X, p 648.

3 T. Morin, *Essai sur l'organisation du travail et l'avenir des classes
   laborieuses*, Paris, 1845, p 1.

4　P. Leroux, *De la ploutocratie ou du gouvernement des riches*, Paris, 1848, p 181.

5　C. Dupont-White, *Essai sur les relations du travail avec le capital*, Paris, 1846, p 433.

6　*Plan de réforme à introduire dans l'organisation du travail*, Paris, 1844, p 39.

7　Quoted in H. Rigandias-Weiss, *Les enquêtes ouvrières en France entre 1830 et 1848*, Paris, 1936, p 238.

8　Cf. the bibliography of bourgeois literature on the condition of workers which appeared between the years 1820 and 1850, by Ruth Hoppe, in J. Kuczynski, op. cit., Vol IX.

9　Inspired by Lenin's work, a few books appeared on the early history of Russian capitalism, e.g. the works of S. G. Strumilin, but none of these is specifically devoted to the Industrial Revolution either.

10　The speech appeared in extended form in the *Zeitschrift für Geschichtswissenschaft*, Berlin, 1956, Book III; in the *Cahiers internationaux*, Paris, 1956, and in an improved version in my *Studien zur Geschichte des Kapitalismus*, Berlin, 1957.

11　For more extensive treatment of this problem, cf. J. Kuczynski, op. cit., p 11ff.

12　London, 1963.

Acknowledgments

The author and publishers would like to thank Mrs Georgina Bruckner who collected the photographs, and the following sources (the number refers to the page on which the illustration appears): Frontispiece The Mansell Collection; 8, 13, 16–17, 19, 27, 31, 36 The British Museum; 9, 20, 21, 23, 28, 29, 33, 47 *top*, 50, 51, 60, 62, 66 *top* and *bottom*, 69, 79, 91, 97, 104, 107, 128, 131, 137, 141, 144, 148, 149, 151, 155 *top* and *bottom*, 157 *top* and *bottom*, 162, 167, 168, 170, 172, 173, 178, 182, 183, 188, 203, 211, 217 The British British Museum, photo by John R. Freeman; 24 Rijksmuseum Kröller Müller, Otterlo; 44, 46, 47 *bottom*, 48–49 (Crown Copyright) The Science Museum; 54, 117, 119, 134, 220 Deutsche Fotothek, Dresden; 71 The Wellcome Historical Medical Library; 84 *top* and *bottom*, 138, 186, 187, 194, 195, 198 Bibliothèque Nationale, Paris, photo by Françoise Foliot; 87, 88, 192 J.E.Bulloz, Paris; 123 The Trades Union Congress, photo by John R. Freeman; 126 The National Portrait Gallery; 200 Rheinisches Bildarchiv, Cologne.

Index

251

252

Mayhew, H. 100,107
Melbourne 221
Mellor 70
Meyer, J. 127
Michel, E. 68,69,74
Michelet, J. 124
Mitchell, D.W. 163
Mohl, M. 105
Moravia 22,216
Morogues 227
Morris, R.B. 173,174
Möser, J. 26,28
Müller, A. 52
Müller, O. 202
Mundt, T. 85,87
Munich 99,159
Murphy, W.E. 221
Murray, C.A. 166
Mysore 223, 224

Nantes 159
Napoleon I 196
Naudet 228
Negroes 72,169–76
Newbury, Jack of 7
Newcastle, Duke of 57
Newcomen, T. 44
New England, 62,72,96,120,
  164,176,177,178,179,218
New Hampshire 120,177
New Jersey 62,67
New Lanark 70
New York 31,62,101,121,
  159,160,169,170,171
New Zealand 140
Nicholls, G. 70
Nisard, D. 43
Northumberland 124
Norway 216
Nottingham 74,132
Nuremberg 31

Oldknow, S. 70
Ortes, G. 37
Owen, R. 126,132,185

Page Arnot, R. 25
Palatinate 173

Palmer 129
Paris 28,30,100,101,160,188,
  190,193,196,218
Paterson 62
Paul, H. 46,212
Pawtucket 120
Pendleton 106
Pennsylvania 62
Philadelphia 31,62,121,159
Phillip,Capt A. 219
Picardy 18
Pittsburg 121,159
Place, F. 126
Plauen 58
Poland 22
Pope, A. 147
Précorbin, de 228
Proudhon, P.J. 192
Prussia 20,22,99,171,208,
  212,218
Prutz, R. 229
Purš 231

Quesnay 187

Raabe, von 21
Redford, A. 69
Rennes 31
Rhode Island 63,120
Ricardo, D. 11,90,130
Richmond 130
Robertson, Rev F.W. 132
Robespierre 14,15,30,185,
  189,199
Rochdale 124
Rolfe 169
Rome 193
Rothenburg-ob-der-Tauber
  81
Rouen 159
Roux, J. 185
Russia, 102,193,202,216–19,
  225,231

Sachsen-Meiningen 83
Saint-Antoine 30
St Étienne 190
Saint-Just, L. 185

St Louis 159
Saint-Simon, L. 186,187,189
Salin, E. 133
San Domingo 76
Sandor, V. 231
Savery 44
Saxony 17,21,53,58
Schleiermacher, F. 43
Schmoller, G. 29,30
Scotland 35,158
Scott, Sir W. 55
Sée, H. 18,70,117,196,197
Seidel, H. 36,37
Seine 196
Seine-Inférieure 195
Sheridan, R. 118
Simon, H. 204
Singh, R. 224
Skipton 130
South Africa 75
Southey, A. 55
Spain 146,202
Spandau 20
Stalin, J. 217
Steward, I. 144,117
Sweden 75,216
Swift, J. 147,149
Switzerland 16
Sydney 219

Tapiès, F.de 98
Tarle, E. 198
Tartary 76
Taylor, W.C. 80,92
Tennyson, A.,Lord 101
Thackeray, W.M. 227
Thompson, E.P. 55,232
Thuringia 32,214
Torgau 21
Toulouse 190
Toynbee, A. 142,230,231
Trevelyan, G.M. 153
Tristan, Flora 190

United States of America 11,
  30,31,35,57,60,61,72,73,
  101,108,114,117,121,125,

World University Library

Some books published or in preparation

Economics and Social Studies

The World Cities
Peter Hall, *London*

The Economics of Underdeveloped Countries
Jagdish Bhagwati, *Delhi*

Development Planning
Jan Tinbergen, *Rotterdam*

Leadership in New Nations
T. B. Bottomore, *Vancouver*

Human Communication
J. L. Aranguren, *Madrid*

Education in the Modern World
John Vaizey, *London*

Soviet Economics
Michael Kaser, *Oxford*

Decisive Forces in World Economics
J. L. Sampedro, *Madrid*

Money
Roger Opie, *Oxford*

The Sociology of Africa
Georges Balandier, *Paris*

Science and Anti-Science
T. R. Gerholm, *Stockholm*

Key Issues in Criminology
Roger Hood, *Durham*

Society and Population
E. A. Wrigley, *Cambridge*

History

The Old Stone Age
François Bordes, *Bordeaux*

The Evolution of Ancient Egypt
Werner Kaiser, *Berlin*

The Emergence of Greek Democracy
W. G. Forrest, *Oxford*

The Roman Empire
J. P. V. D. Balsdon, *Oxford*

Muhammad and the Conquests of Islam
Francesco Gabrieli, *Rome*

The Age of Charlemagne
Jacques Boussard, *Poitiers*

The Crusades
Geo Widengren, *Uppsala*

The Medieval Economy
Georges Duby, *Aix-en-Provence*

The Medieval Italian Republics
D. P. Waley, *London*

The Ottoman Empire
Halil Inalcik, *Ankara*

Humanism in the Renaissance
S. Dresden, *Leyden*

The Rise of Toleration
Henry Kamen, *Warwick*

The Left in Europe since 1789
David Caute, *Oxford*

The Rise of the Working Class
Jürgen Kuczynski, *Berlin*

Chinese Communism
Robert North, *Stanford*

Arab Nationalism
Sylvia Haim, *London*

The Culture of Japan
Mifune Okumura, *Kyoto*

The History of Persia
Jean Aubin, *Paris*

Philosophy and Religion

Christianity
W. O. Chadwick, *Cambridge*

Monasticism
David Knowles, *London*

Judaism
J. Soetendorp, *Amsterdam*

The Modern Papacy
K. O. von Aretin, *Göttingen*

Sects
Bryan Wilson, *Oxford*

Language and Literature

A Model of Language
E. M. Uhlenbeck, *Leyden*

French Literature
Raymond Picard, *Paris*

Russian Writers and Society 1825–1904
Ronald Hingley, *Oxford*

Satire
Matthew Hodgart, *Sussex*

The Romantic Century
Robert Baldick, *Oxford*

The Arts

The Language of Modern Art
Ulf Linde, *Stockholm*

Architecture since 1945
Bruno Zevi, *Rome*

Twentieth Century Music
H. H. Stuckenschmidt, *Berlin*

Aesthetic Theories since 1850
J. F. Revel, *Paris*

Art Nouveau
S. Tschudi Madsen, *Oslo*

Academic Painting
Gerald Ackerman, *Stanford*

Palaeolithic Cave Art
P. J. Ucko and A. Rosenfeld, *London*

Primitive Art
Eike Haberland, *Mainz*

Romanesque Art
Carlos Cid Priego, *Madrid*

Expressionism
John Willett, *London*

Psychology and Human Biology

The Molecules of Life
Gisela Nass, *Munich*

The Variety of Man
J. P. Garlick, *London*

Eye and Brain
R. L. Gregory, *Cambridge*

The Ear and the Brain
E. C. Carterette, *U.C.L.A.*

The Biology of Work
O. G. Edholm, *London*

The Psychology of Attention
Anne Treisman, *Oxford*

Psychoses
H. J. Bochnik, *Hamburg*

Psychosomatic Medicine
A. Mitscherlich, *Heidelberg*

Child Development
Phillipe Muller, *Neuchâtel*

Man and Disease
Gernot Rath, *Göttingen*

Chinese Medicine
P. Huard and M. Wong, *Paris*

Mind in the Universe
Gösta Ehrensvärd, *Lund*

Zoology and Botany

The Age of the Dinosaurs
Björn Kurtén, *Helsingfors*

Animal Communication
J. M. Cullen, *Oxford*

Mimicry
Wolfgang Wickler, *Seewiesen*

Migration
Gustaf Rudebeck, *Stockholm*

Lower Animals
Martin Wells, *Cambridge*

The World of an Insect
Rémy Chauvin, *Strasbourg*

Biological Rhythms
Janet Harker, *Cambridge*

Life in the Sea
Gunnar Thorson, *Helsingore*

Primates
François Bourlière, *Paris*

The Conservation of Nature
C. Delamare Deboutteville, *Paris*

The Variation of Plants
S. M. Walters and D. Briggs,
Cambridge

Physical Science and Mathematics

Energy
Etienne Fischhoff, *Paris*

Crystals and Minerals
Hugo Strunz, *Berlin*

The Quest for Absolute Zero
K. Mendelssohn, *Oxford*

Particles and Accelerators
Robert Gouiran, *C.E.R.N., Geneva*

What is Light?
A. C. S. van Heel and C. H. F. Velzel,
Eindhoven

Waves and Corpuscles
J. A. e Silva and G. Lochak, *Paris*
Introduction by Louis de Broglie

Mathematics Observed
H. Freudenthal, *Utrecht*

Science and Statistics
S. Sagoroff, *Vienna*

Earth Sciences and Astronomy

The Structure of the Universe
E. L. Schatzman, *Paris*

Climate and Weather
H. Flohn, *Bonn*

Anatomy of the Earth
André Cailleux, *Paris*

The Electrical Earth
J. Sayers, *Birmingham*

Applied Science

Words and Waves
A. H. W. Beck, *Cambridge*

The Science of Decision-making
A. Kaufmann, *Paris*

Bionics
Lucien Gérardin, *Paris*

Metals and Civilisation
R. W. Cahn, *Sussex*

Bioengineering
H. S. Wolff, *London*